Paul W. Holland

THE STRUCTURE OF POSITIVE SENTIMENT

Progress in
Mathematical Social Sciences

Volume 6

THE STRUCTURE
OF
POSITIVE SENTIMENT

MAUREEN T. HALLINAN

Department of Sociology,
University of Wisconsin, Madison

 Elsevier Scientific Publishing Company

Amsterdam · London · New York 1974

For the U.S.A. and Canada
AMERICAN ELSEVIER PUBLISHING COMPANY, INC.
52 VANDERBILT AVENUE
NEW YORK, NEW YORK 10017

For all other areas
ELSEVIER SCIENTIFIC PUBLISHING COMPANY
335 JAN VAN GALENSTRAAT
P.O. BOX 211, AMSTERDAM, THE NETHERLANDS

With 10 illustrations and 22 tables

Library of Congress Card Number: 73-90960

ISBN 0-444-41197-6

Copyright © 1974 by Elsevier Scientific Publishing Company, Amsterdam
All rights reserved. No part of this publication may be reproduced, stored in a
retrieval system, or transmitted in any form or by any means, electronic, mechan-
ical, photocopying, recording, or otherwise, without the prior written permission of
the publisher.
Elsevier Scientific Publishing Company, Jan van Galenstraat 335, Amsterdam

Printed in The Netherlands

Progress in Mathematical Social Sciences

EDITORS:

Raymond Boudon, *Université René Descartes, Sorbonne − Paris*
David D. McFarland, *University of Chicago*

ADVISORY BOARD:

Marc Barbut, *Paris*
D.J. Bartholomew, *London School of Economics*
Brian J.L. Berry, *University of Chicago*
Vittorio Capecchi, *Bologna*
James S. Coleman, *University of Chicago*
Philip E. Converse, *University of Michigan*
Clyde H. Coombs, *University of Michigan*
Patrick Doreian, *University of Pittsburgh*
Claude Flament, *Aix-en-Provence*
Paul Kay, *University of California, Berkeley*
Nathan Keyfitz, *Harvard University*
Paul Lazarsfeld, *University of Pittsburgh*
Judah Matras, *The Hebrew University of Jerusalem*
Jürgen Pelikan, *Vienna*
Anatol Rapoport, *University of Toronto*
Lynne Roberts, *University of California, Berkeley*
Seymour Spilerman, *University of Wisconsin, Madison*
William H. Starbuck, *Berlin*
Patrick Suppes, *Stanford University*
Harrison C. White, *Harvard University*
Gerard de Zeeuw, *University of Amsterdam*

Other books included in this series

Preface

The purpose of this volume is to present and test a mathematical model of the structure of positive sentiment relations in friendship groups. The model has, as its theoretical base, Heider's notions of balanced sentiment relations and further developments in consistency theory, as well as Homans' propositions on group interaction. The formalization of these propositions is in terms of graph theory, and is based on the early Cartwright and Harary model of balance, as well as Davis' more recent model of clusterability, Davis and Leinhardt's ranked clusters model and Holland and Leinhardt's transitivity model. The proposed model, which is a modification of the most general of the previous formulations, the transitivity model, was developed in an attempt to overcome the theoretical weaknesses of the transitivity model and to improve its fit to empirical data.

The modified transitivity model was tested on a sample of 51 groups of school children in grades five through eight. These groups had natural boundaries for social interaction, making them highly appropriate for the analysis. The Holland-Leinhardt transitivity model was tested on the same sample, and the results compared. The new model received strong support in each of the groups and was more successful than the Holland-Leinhardt model in nearly every group. In addition the new model was tested on the Davis-Leinhardt pool of 742 sociomatrices and again received strong support. The success of the modified transitivity model is convincing evidence that sentiment relations tend to be transitive and to possess the structural characteristics which the model depicts.

This book should be of interest to anyone concerned with formalizing verbal theory. In addition, it should appeal to students of group structure and social networks, regardless of the conceptual base of these networks. Methodologists who reject the unsystematic, descriptive analyses of sociograms which fill the literature may find the proposed model a more appropriate method of studying social interaction from a group rather than an individualistic perspective. Finally, the study should provide a better understanding of social relationships to support the intuitive fears of many psychologists, sociologists and educators who hesitate to use sociometric data to alter group structure for therapeutic purposes.

The author gratefully acknowledges support by National Science Foundation Grant GP-30327 and computing time made available by the University of Chicago. She also wishes to express her sincere gratitude to the several persons who assisted her in the present study. Edwin Bridges played a major role in helping conceptualize and organize the research. David McFarland provided valuable insights at various stages of the work. Thomas Pullum gave important advice concerning the statistical measures and John Glidewell made helpful suggestions for improving drafts. The study could not have been conducted without the important contribution of Maurice J. Moore who acted as computer consultant. The work was made considerably easier by Josephine Rooney who coded the data and Richard Nault who edited and typed parts of the manuscript. Finally, special thanks are due to the principals, teachers and children who generously provided the data for the study.

Contents

CHAPTER I

The Transitivity Model

The term structure is one of the most frequently used concepts in sociological theory. Social structure, communication structure, and attitude structure are familiar terms. But despite the extensive use of such concepts, a precise definition of structure is seldom found. As a consequence, descriptions of structural properties tend to be ambiguous and actual studies of structure, as such, are seldom found.

One of the few attempts to define social structure rigorously was made by Siegfried Nadel (1956). In his highly theoretical work, Nadel distinguishes between social order and social structure. Social order emerges as ongoing relationships among social actors become interwoven into relatively stable and predictable arrangements. It exists whenever social interactions become patterned and recurrent. Social order is often stable, but it is never static. In order to describe social order it is necessary to "freeze" it and to refer to isolated instances of the continually flowing process. Social structure is always a static, unvarying configuration of social relationships. It is the arrangement of configuration of social activities, attitudes or sentiments that is seen to exist over some period of time and that is believed to depict patterns of social order. One arrives at the structure of a group through abstracting from the concrete population and its behavior the pattern or network of relationships obtaining between actors in their capacity of playing roles relative to one another.

Nadel's definition of social structure can be applied to the structure of sentiment relations in small groups. The sentiment structure of a friendship group is the arrangement of sentiment relations which one observes over time and which depicts patterns of regularity. Sentiment structure exists not in the sentiments of the actors themselves but in the observed uniformities of recurrent patterns of sentiment that transpire among the actors over time. The study of sentiment structure involves the detection of these patterns and the discovery of the social laws which explain them.

Laws of social behavior which explain patterns of regularity and determine structure apply to all individuals in a group regardless of the personalities involved. This accounts for similarity in the structure of different groups. If such laws were to apply to small-scale sentiment groups, they would limit some kinds of sentiment relations and provide opportunities for other kinds. A network of sentiments, independent of individual personalities, would emerge. This network would create a single sentiment structure which one could expect to find in all small-scale sentiment groups.

The most frequently used method of studying sentiment structure in small groups is found in sociometry. The term sociometry refers to the study and measurement of interpersonal relations in a group of people. The sociometric method consists of asking members of a group to choose other members according to some criterion, such as preferred seating companion or preferred playmate. Sociometric questionnaires differ only in terms of the sociometric criterion used and the number of responses permitted. Subjects are classified as stars, above average, below average, neglectees, and rejectees based on the frequency of choices viewed. The distribution of choices is pictured graphically by a sociogram or a sociomatrix and this diagram is said to represent the social structure of the group.

In addition to data on the distribution of choices, most sociometric studies contain a collection of information on the psychological and social class characteristics of individual group members. The studies relate these attributes to the choice distribution and draw conclusions about their effect on social position. Sociometry's main contribution, therefore, lies in the insights it offers into the interrelations between these characteristics of a person and his place in the social structure.

While there is obvious value in discovering what variables affect social acceptance, this approach contains little of structural significance. When subjected to scrutiny, the traditional sociometric approach is found to contain a naive, intuitive concept of structure. This concept contains implicit assumptions about group structure which are highly questionable. These assumptions are found in (1) an individualistic perspective, (2) a mono-clique ideal, and (3) a dependence on visual analysis.

(1) *Individualistic perspective.* Most sociometric studies consist of a correlation between behavioral and personality characteristics of group members and their place (star, neglectee, rejectee) in the social system. The personal and social characteristics of individuals are seen as the determinants of social structure. The variables most frequently correlated with social structure are identified by Glidewell (Glidewell *et al.*, 1965) in his extensive review of the literature on social structure. The following sample from his list illustrates the preponderance of studies of this type:[1]

Physical fitness — Force, 1954; Whaley, 1954; Woronaff, 1954.

Intelligence — Long, 1959; Kuhlen and Lee, 1943; Young and Cooper, 1944; Potashin, 1946; Shoobs, 1947; Grossman and Wrighter, 1948; Laughlin, 1954; Van Egmond, 1960.

Social-emotional adjustment — Bonney, 1943; Baron, 1951; Tagiuri, 1952; Rehage, 1951; Bower, 1957; Lippit and Gold, 1959.

Social class — Bonney, 1942; Neugarten, 1946; Grossman and Wrighter, 1948; Wilson, 1959.

This approach assumes that social structure is an accumulation of personality types. It implies that actors are free of group constraints and that personal variables, not interlocking group relations, determine social behavior. However, group structure emerges when individuals, acting as part of social relationships, create patterns of social order. These patterns become realities distinct from the individual actors and therefore are independent of the personalities involved. Categorizing individuals with respect to a group or determining what variables affect behavior say nothing about these interrelationships which form patterns of regularity. Consequently, such studies do not truly deal with group structure.

(2) *Mono-clique ideal.* The traditional sociometric approach to social structure contains an implicit assumption about the ideal organization of a group. The manner in which behavior is categorized and stereotyped reveals the assumption that the ideal group is one in which each member is engaged in mutual choice relations with every other member. One is led to believe that everyone ought to be a leader and no one should be an isolate. The implications of this assumption are that hierarchies and cleavages in a group, even sex cleavages, represent a deviation from the ideal and interfere with the social integration of the group. This assumption of a mono-clique structure completely neglects the possibility that underlying patterns of behavior might produce an alternate organization as ideal or natural. The assumption merits severe criticism because it assumes that which is to be investigated, namely, the structure of the group.

Besides being an unrecognized, and therefore untested assumption, the widespread belief that the ideal group is not fragmented by cliques and hierarchy has dangerous implications. Sociometrics was originally proposed by Moreno as a guide to psychotherapy. This idea became popular and soon sociometric studies, especially in education, were performed with a therapeutic intent. Since mutuality was the ideal, clique boundaries had to be broken down. Since status was identified with non-mutual or asymmetric relations, it too was excluded. Improved social relations, it was believed, would result from discouraging both cliques and status hierarchies, and efforts were made to achieve this goal. However, if underlying laws of sentiment relations should determine a structure which allows both cliques and hierarchy, efforts to model a group on a mono-clique structure would, at best, be temporarily successful, and at worst, dysfunctional or even damaging to the group. Given the delicate nature of psychotherapy, even in its most limited application, it is necessary to have firm notions of structure before attempting to change people's behavior or their relationships to each other.

(3) *Visual analysis.* Sociometric studies assume that social structure can be detected solely by visual analysis. This assumption is easily rejected. Sociograms defy visual ordering in any but the simplest cases. Ranking systems and cliques are not easy to detect in a sociogram except in small groups; interrelationships are far

from visible. Yet, the belief that a sociogram is a picture of the social structure of a group is prevalent. It is a picture, but only one among the many possible representations which could be drawn of a group. There are no rules for its manipulation, no guidelines to decide which picture reveals the "true" structure of the group. The diagram lacks the power to portray any but the simplest relationships of individuals to the group.

Even if the sociogram were more adequate as a visual description of sentiment structure, it would still lack the power to detect the patterns of relations which actually determine the structure of the group. A two-dimensional design cannot portray complex configurations of relationships. Moreover, a sociogram may become an obstacle to the detection of structure by distorting these patterns. The only appropriate techniques for examining structure must have the power to reveal the patterns which determine structure as well as simple descriptive properties associated with it.

The above analysis establishes the position that traditional methods of detecting sentiment structure are inadequate. While the studies mentioned yield important results, they do not accomplish what they so often purport to do, namely, reveal structure. The complexity of group structure demands a more powerful methodology to analyze it. The present study seeks to respond to that need.

A Graph Theoretic Approach

A promising trend is developing in the field of social science in the use of mathematical theories to provide models of social behavior. Markov chains, matrix algebra, abstract algebra, game theory and differential equations have been used to great advantage in the study of social phenomena. As demonstrated by these studies, formalization adds clarity, precision and predictive power to verbal theory.

Two mathematical theories in particular, algebra and graph theory, have achieved prominence as useful means to formalize theories of interpersonal sentiment. The algebraic approach holds attraction for the mathematically sophisticated but graph theory has achieved greater popularity because of its simplicity and the closeness of its concepts to corresponding sociological ones.

Graph theory is concerned with patterns of relationships among pairs of abstract elements and, as such, serves as a mathematical model of the structural properties of any empirical system consisting of relationships among pairs of elements. There are two slightly different approaches to graph theory, one using signed graphs and the other diagraphs. In a signed graph, all of the points in the set are connected by lines which are designated as positive or negative. A digraph contains direct lines between a subset of points in the set. Since signed graphs can be transformed into digraphs and since digraphs are conceptually close to the empirical situation being investigated, the latter approach is taken in the present study.

The undefined terms, or primitives, of digraph theory are:

P_1 : A set of X elements called "points".

P_2 : A set V of elements called "line segments".

P_3 : A function f whose domain is V and whose range is contained in X.

P_4 : A function s whose domain is V and whose range is contained in X.

The axioms are:

A_1 : The set X is finite, and not empty.

A_2 : $\left. \begin{array}{l} f(v_1) = f(v_2) \\ \\ s(v_1) = s(v_2) \end{array} \right\} \implies v_1 = v_2$

that is, no distinct line segments are parallel (have the same initial points and the same terminal points).

A_3 : There exists no v such that f(v) = s(v) that is, there are no loops (line segments whose initial and terminal points are identical).

In using digraph theory to provide a model of the structure of interpersonal relations the following isomorphism between the primitives of the graph-theoretic axiomatic system and concepts in the empirical social system is made:

point ⟷ person

line segment ⟷ friendship relation between two persons as determined by choice on a sociometric test.

f ⟷ function which associates the friendship relation with the chooser on a sociometric test.

s   ———————▶ function which associates the friendship relation with the person chosen on a socio-metric test.

The isomorphism establishes the empirical relation of friendship on a set of people X. The relation consists of a set of ordered pairs of people such that (x_1, x_2) is in the relation if and only if x_1 chooses x_2 as his friend. The presence of a line v in a sociogram and the relation $f(v) = x_1$ and $s(v) = x_2$ implies that the person corresponding to point x_1 chooses the person corresponding the x_2 while the absence of such a line and corresponding relation means the x_1 does not choose x_2 on a sociometric test. The axioms are translated as follows:

A_1 : V contains a finite number of people and is not empty.

A_2 : A person cannot choose another person more than once in response to a sociometric question.

A_3 : A person cannot choose himself in response to a socio-metric question. (This axiom does not exclude a person's liking himself but merely from expressing that sentiment on the sociometric test.)

The first graph-theoretic model of structure in interpersonal relations to be postulated was Cartwright and Harary's model of structural balance (Cartwright and Harary, 1956). Cartwright and Harary employed signed graphs for their model. In signed graph theory a cycle is a set of distinct points $(x_1, x_2, \ldots x_n)$ and a closed sequence of lines $(v_1, v_2, \ldots v_n)$ such that v_i connects x_i and x_{i+1} for $1 \leqslant i < n$ and v_n connects x_n and x_1. A graph is balanced if and only if its points can be separated into two mutual-ly exclusive subsets such that each positive line joins two points of the same subset and each negative line joins two points from dif-ferent subsets. The model is built on the structure theorem which states that a graph is divided into two cliques (balanced) if and only if it has no cycles with an odd number of negative lines.

Davis' clustering model (Davis, 1967) generalized the notion of balance to a number of clusters or cliques by utilizing a theorem which states that a graph is clusterable if and only if it has no cycles containing a single negative line. Since unity is an odd num-ber, balance is a special case of clusterability.

Building on this foundation, but using digraphs rather than signed graphs, Davis and Leinhardt developed a model of ranked

7

clusters (Davis and Leinhardt, 1972). The model is based on Homans' proposition that small groups inevitably generate a social structure which combines subgroups (cliques) and a ranking system. Some empirical support was found for the model in a large collection of sociograms gathered from diverse sources.

An analysis of empirical data which provided some support for the ranked clusters model led to the development, by Holland and Leinhardt (Holland and Leinhardt, 1971), of the more generalized transitivity model. This model, also formulated in terms of digraphs, is built around the mathematical concept of a partially ordered set. It describes a class of structural models all of which satisfy at least the minimal conditions defining a partial order. Both Cartwright and Harary's model of structural balance when translated into digraphs, and Davis' model of clusterability satisfy these conditions as does the ranked clusters model of Davis and Leinhardt. Consequently, all of these models are special cases of the transitivity model. The additional condition placed on the ranked clusters model allows the existence of only one hierarchy whereas the transitivity model contains more than one.

All of these graph theoretic models are stated in strong deterministic fashion. As they stand, the theorems allow no exceptions, and graphs in which only one cycle fails to meet the criterion are, strictly speaking, as incorrect as those with many failures. Since empirical data always will have exceptions, it is necessary to develop probabilistic models to assess degree of clusterability and hierarchy. Harary (Harary, 1959) was the first to propose such a statistical model for balance. Davis and Leinhardt (Davis and Leinhardt, 1972) suggested a probablistic model for measuring approximation to their ranked clusters model while Holland and Leinhardt (Holland and Leinhardt, 1970) developed a powerful statistical model to measure significant tendencies toward the transitivity model.

Statement of the Transitivity Model

The basic components of the transitivity model are the set X of elements x, y, . . . , together with a binary relation C defined on X such that $(x, y) \epsilon$ C if and only if there exists a v such that $f(v) = x$ and $s(v) = y$. In other words, x C y if and only if a directed line segment goes from x to y, or empirically, if and only if person x chooses person y on a sociometric test. C defines three relations on X. These are:

(1) x M y if and only if x C y and y C x
(2) x A y if and only if x C y and not y C x
(3) x N y if and only if neither x C y nor y C x

The sociometric interpretation of these relations is mutual, asymetric and null relations between two persons in a group.

Definition 1: (X, C) is a partially ordered set (poset) if and only if for all x, y, z ε X
(a) x C x
(b) x C y and y C z implies that x C z.

Some authors define a poset as being antisymmetric as well as reflexive and transitive. The following definition of antisymmetry demonstrates that it can be derived from the other two properties.

Definition 2: R is antisymmetric with respect to an equivalence relation[2] E, if and only if for all x, y ε X:
x R y and y R x ⇒ x E y

In (X, C) x C y and y C x ⇒ x M y where M is an equivalence relation. Hence the reflexivity and transitivity of C imply its antisymmetry.

A second point to be noted is that property (a) of a poset, reflexivity, contradicts axiom 3 for digraphs which states that a digraph is irreflexive, that is, contains no loops. Despite this contradiction it is possible to apply digraph theory to posets by making the following accommodation. Let poset (X, C) correspond to digraph (X, C′) where

(a) for x ≠ y, x C′ y if and only if x C y, and
(b) there exists no x such that x C′ x.

The structural properties of (X, C) which are of interest in this study are the same as those of (X, C′). The reflexive property of the poset, while eliminating trivial special cases and providing the harmless psychological assumption that a person likes himself, has no effect on the structural properties of the set. This allows the use of digraphs to analyze posets.

The three theorems on which Holland and Leinhardt build their transitivity model will be stated without proof as follows:

9

Theorem 1:   If (X, C) is a poset, then for all x, y, z in X:
    (a) x M x
    (b) x M y implies that y M x
    (c) x M y and y M z implies that x M z
    (d) x A y implies not y A x
    (e) x A y and y A z implies x A z
    (f) not x N x
    (g) x N y implies that y N x.

Theorem 1 implies that M is an equivalence relation on X which partitions X into a system of mutually exclusive and exhaustive subsets (M-cliques) with the property that x and y are in the same subset if and only if x M y. The sociological implication is that two persons are members of the same clique if and only if they are involved in a mutual choice relation.

Theorem 2:   If (X, C) is a poset and if u M v, then for all x belonging to X:
    (a) u A x if and only if v A x
    (b) x A u if and only if x A v
    (c) u N x if and only if v N x.

Theorem 2 implies that all elements of an M-clique are structurally identical, that is, they stand in the same relation to any other element of X.

Definition 3:   If U and V are two distinct M-cliques of X, then U C* V if and only if u A v for all u in U and v in V. Also, set U C* U for all M-cliques, U.

The ordering relation C* establishes a transitive hierarchy of cliques when individuals in different cliques are linked by A relations. Thus asymmetric pairs indicate a status differential in which the chosen individual possesses higher status than the chooser.

Theorems 1 and 2 contain implicitly the essential graph-theoretic properties of the transitivity model. These are made explicit in theorem 3.

Theorem 3:   If (X, C) is a poset, then the elements of X may be partitioned into disjoint subsets (the M-cliques) which have the following properties:
    (a) Within each subset all pairs of elements are jointed by M-edges (all clique members like and

are liked by all other members of the same clique);

(b) Between any two given, distinct subsets all pairs of elements are either all joined by A-edges with the same direction or all joined by N-edges (cliques may or may not be ordered, if they are not ordered then they are disconnected);

(c) The subsets, when ordered by C*, form a poset that is also antisymmetric (cliques may be collapsed to points without affecting status).

For a given set of points, to verify whether or not C is transitive, every ordered triple of distinct elements (x, y, z) must be examined. Triads are labeled by three numerals referring, respectively, to the number of M, A, and N-edges they contain. For example, the 0-1-2 triad contains no mutual, one asymmetric and two null relations. No distinction is made among the permutations of the elements in an ordered triple, so that the following configurations are all classified as 0-1-2 triads:

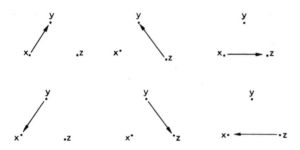

Fig. 1. Configurations of the 0-2-1 triad.

A triad is intransitive if for at least one of the ordered triples of individuals that make it up, say (x, y, z), it occurs that x C y and y C z but not x C z. Thus, a triad may be intransitive from the perspective of one, two or all three of the individuals that comprise it. On the other hand, if any of the following situations holds:

x C y and not y C z

not x C y but y C z

neither x C y nor y C z

11

then the transitivity condition says nothing regarding x C z or not x C z. These triplets are called vacuously transitive. Figure 2 represents the triads as they are arranged by Holland and Leinhardt.

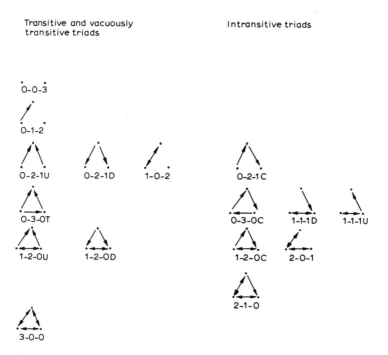

Transitive and vacuously
transitive triads

Intransitive triads

0-0-3

0-1-2

0-2-1U   0-2-1D   1-0-2   0-2-1C

0-3-OT   0-3-OC   1-1-1D   1-1-1U

1-2-OU   1-2-OD   1-2-OC   2-0-1

                                  2-1-0

3-0-0

Fig. 2. All 16 triad types arranged horizontally by number of choices made and divided vertically into those with at least one intransitivity and those with no intransitivities.

The heart of the transitivity model lies in Theorem 3 which implies that a directed graph may be arranged into disjoint systems of ranked clusters of cliques if and only if it does not contain any of the intransitive triads. The strength of the theorem is that it allows one to identify group structure by examining properties of components of the group; a far more manageable endeavor. The theorem establishes that the absence of non-permissible triads in a group implies a network of sentiment relations which has the total structure described, namely, hierarchies of ranked clusters of cliques.

The ranked clusters model contains an additional assumption which has the effect of limiting the number of possible structural arrangements. While a poset may contain disconnected components yielding a number of hierarchies, a system of ranked clusters can possess only one. A necessary and sufficient condition for the ranked clusters structure is the absence of both the intransitive triads and the 0-1-2 triad from the graph. Other special cases of the poset, obtained by additional assumptions, include the balance model, the clusterability model, transitive tournaments, quasi-series, completely connected groups and single star structure.

Theoretical Background

Choice of the transitivity model as the structural model for networks of positive interpersonal sentiment demands justification. Why postulate that the structure of sentiment relations is hierarchies of ranked clusters of cliques rather than a number of other possible structures such as a transitive tournament, a single-star structure or a mono-clique? In turning to social science literature to find a plausible theoretical foundation for the model, one discovers both psychological and sociological theories and empirical studies supporting it. Psychological consistency theories offer support for the principle of transitivity of sentiment while sociological theories of interaction predict the existence of cliques and a hierarchical system in friendship groups. Since it has been proven by graph theory that the ranked clusters structure exists if and only if the choice relation is transitive, both analyses provide support for the model.

Transitivity of Sentiment

The three major consistency formulations are congruity (Osgood and Tannenbaum, 1965), balance (Heider, 1946; Newcomb, 1953; Abelson and Rosenberg, 1958) and dissonance (Festinger, 1958). The differences in the three are minimal and it has been shown that their mathematical structures are fundamentally the same. Balance theory is more amenable to studies of interpersonal relations and it is used here to provide the psychological rationale for transitivity of sentiment.

Heider's theory of balance identifies states of balance and imbalance in the cognitive field of an experiencing person p, as he relates to another person o, and to some attitudinal object x. The relations are of two kinds: a positive or negative attitude and a unit relation involved in perceiving persons or objects as belonging together in a specially close way. Using signed graphs, Cartwright and Harary (Cartwright and Harary, 1956) depict an unbalanced situation as follows:

> p likes o (+)
> o tells a lie (+ unit relation between o and x)
> p disapproves of lying (− relation between p and x)

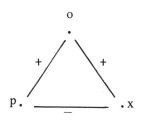

The above cognitive situation would become balanced if p were to dislike o, if p were to sever the unit relation between o and x (it isn't typical of o to lie) or if p were to dissolve the experience unity of o by introducing a cognitive differentiation that segregates the aspect of o as liar (disliked) from the rest of o (liked), both differentiated aspects then entering into balanced triads. One notes that the graph of an unbalanced situation has an odd number of negative lines while the graph of a balanced one has an even number.

Newcomb proposed a slightly modified version of the theory under which p-o-x relations are subjectively balanced. The significance of the new version is that it extended the theory to include interpersonal sentiments as well as cognitions. Abelson and Resenberg further extended p-o-x to encompass more general conditions of consistency within and between cognitions about an emotionally significant issue.

To apply balance theory to transitivity of sentiment one must translate from signed graphs into digraphs. This can be done by interpreting a positive line segment as a directed arrow and both a negative line segment and the absence of a line segment as the absence of an arrow. Since triads are balanced with respect to a person, that is, in the mind or psychological field of a person, p, one can concentrate on p's sentiments toward O_1 and O_2 and ignore the reciprocal relations implicit in signed graphs. Consider the following situation:

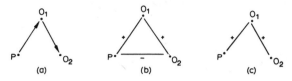

Fig. 3. Translation of digraph representation of 0-2-1C triad (a) into signed graphs (b) & (c).

If the absence of $\overrightarrow{PO_2}$ (a) represents a negative line in a signed graph as in (b), the $P-O_1-O_2$ triad has an odd number of negative lines and is unbalanced. Balance would be restored by replacing P's negative sentiments toward O_2 by positive ones. Using digraphs this would call for the directed arrow $\overrightarrow{PO_2}$ which is the same as demanding transitivity of sentiment. If the absence of $\overrightarrow{PO_2}$ is interpreted as the absence of a signed line (c), then balance theory is not applicable and offers no reason for demanding the existence of $\overrightarrow{PO_2}$ or sentimental transitivity. The occurrence of the empirical situation depicted by (c) may be infrequent, however, since intuitively it seems unlikely that a person will entertain no sentiment toward another person whom he knows.

While consistency theory cannot explain the absence of all the triangular configurations classified as non-permissible in the transitivity model, it does predict the infrequent occurrence of most of the intransitive triads, because they imply unbalanced or distressful situations. In this way psychological theory lends strong support to the transitivity model.

Most of the empirical research which has been done to discover whether interpersonal sentiments conform to consistency models use perceived sentiments as the dependent variable, not extant interpersonal sentiments.[3] There are, however, three published studies which address the issue of actual sentimental consistency. Kogan and Tagiuri (Kogan and Tagiuri, 1958) showed that Heider's hypotheses are supported by the sociometric choices of a group of 22 naval enlisted men. White (White, 1961) used the Abelson and Rosenberg theory to describe the sociometric choices of a group of 16 industrial executives. Newcomb's study (New-

15

comb, 1961) of college students in an experimental residence showed that as interpersonal relations stabilized in established social groups they approximate conditions of objective balance in which people who share agreement about important issues and feel the same way about other people also come to like each other. The outcomes of these three studies were predicted by consistency theory and illustrate its relevance to transitivity of sentiment.

Cliques

While psychological consistency theory offers an explanation for transitivity, sociological theory addresses itself to the formation of the structure which results from the transitivity principle, namely, hierarchies of ranked cliques. Homans' well-known relationship between social interaction and interpersonal sentiments is a widely accepted explanation of clique formation (Homans, 1950). He reasons that differential frequencies of interaction and interpersonal liking and similarity in other sentiments and activities go together. As a consequence, pairs and larger subsets come to be increasingly differentiated from the rest of the group forming cliques characterized by high rates of voluntary interaction, positive interpersonal sentiments and normative concensus.[4]

Homans' notion of the external system also supports the idea of cliques (Homans, 1950). In any group the external system (or group's environment) makes it likely that frequencies of interaction will be unevenly distributed among the members of the group. When organized to get work done or to achieve goals, a group almost always produces clusters of social interaction. The resulting voluntary interaction generates positive sentiments, and strong sentimental cliques result.

Homans' explanation of clique formation is in terms of a prior principle – the need for persons to cluster in order to attain a goal. Several studies (Blake *et al.,* 1956; Gullahorn, 1952; Merton, 1948; Whyte, 1956) demonstrate that even small differences in the microecology of interaction have a strong effect on clique formation. Together with Homans' theory they suggest that the external system is an important factor in creating clique structures.

Empirical studies point to other sociological variables which play a part in clique formation. Coleman (Coleman, 1961) and

Gordon (Gordon, 1957) show that sociometric choices among high school students tend to be concentrated heavily within sex and grade level. Cliquing could be detected in the sociogram of a high school even if choices within a sex and age group were totally random. Other studies reveal that social categories which also play a role in determining cliques are socioeconomic status, family background, intelligence and academic achievement, age and physical development and values and interests. (Bonney, 1942; Cook, Leeds, and Callis, 1951; Hollingshead, 1949; Bonney, 1943; Coleman, 1959; Long, 1958–1959; and Coleman, 1961).

Hierarchy

In support of the hierarchical ordering of cliques, Homans offers another principle. He postulates that group members are more nearly alike in the norms they hold than in their conformity to these norms and since the closer a person's activities come to the norm the higher his rank will be, all groups develop systems of ranking (Homans, 1950). He does not actually define the structure implied by these propositions but his reasoning can be applied to the formulation found in the transitivity model.

After reviewing the literature of the development of structure in school groups, Glidewell (Glidewell *et al.*, 1965) suggests a classroom is made up of a hierarchy of cliques and isolates and that these sub-groups are ordered on the basis of popularity and power. He claims that this kind of hierarchy has often been proposed but is not yet clearly substantiated in empirical findings.

There are some empirical studies which support a hierarchical ordering of cliques. Coleman (Coleman, 1959) pointed to excellence in athletics, school activities, and academics as providing differential status for high school groups. Gordon (Gordon, 1957) demonstrated that while grade achievement of high school students was least significantly related to general status, student organizations served to define status relationships for the whole system. Hollingshead (Hollingshead, 1949) showed that the prestige structure is stratified into classes in both the sentiments and the behavior of the members of the community on the basis of socio-economic factors. Sherif and Sherif (Sherif and Sherif, 1953) found a hierarchy of interlocking cliques in their well-known Robbers Cave Experiment.

17

In summary, psychological consistency theory offers a rationale for postulating transitivity of sentiment while sociological inter-action theories suggest ranked cliques as the structure of friend-ship relations. These theories and the empirical studies based on them provide sufficient justification for choosing the transitivity model as a realistic model of the structure of interpersonal re-lations in small groups.

The Problem

While the formulation of the transitivity model may be regarded as a significant first step toward a rigorous analysis of group struc-ture, the model contains certain weaknesses which limit its useful-ness. The aim of the present research is to eliminate those weak-nesses by modifying and extending the model and by altering the data collection techniques used to test it. The improved model will then be tested on empirical data.

Modification of the Model

A major weakness in the transitivity model lies in its dichot-omization of triads. Classifying triads as intransitive and transitive or vacuously transitive rests on the assumption that all the intran-sitive or non-permissible triads should appear with equal frequen-cy. Consequently, all the triads are given the same weight in the model. Empirical testing has shown that this assumption is not valid (Davis and Leinhardt, 1972). Some of the intransitive triads appear far less frequently than others relative to the predictions of the random model and all the transitive triads appear more fre-quently than the vacuously transitive ones. Holland and Lein-hardt's dichotomy needs refinement to explain this phenomenon.

Another problem inherent in the model's classification of triads is that it does not account for the frequency of the non-permiss-ible 2-1-0 triad. When Davis and Leinhardt first analyzed their data to test their ranked clusters model, they discovered that the 0-1-2 triad and the 2-1-0 triad occurred far more often than their model would predict. Investigation of this problem led Holland and Leinhardt to formulate the transitivity model. By permitting more than one hierarchy, this model explained the occurrence of the

0-1-2 triad and allowed it to be reclassified as permissible. But this still did not solve the problem of the 2-1-0 triad. When Davis (Davis, 1970) turned his attention to the frequent occurrence of this triad, he concluded that there was no graph theoretic model which could classify it as permissible. As a result, its frequent occurrence in group after group remains an enigma, and is the single outstanding source of lack of support for the transitivity model in empirical data.

To solve the problem of the differential frequency of non-permissible and permissible triads and to explain the occurrence of the 2-1-0 triad, a new classification of triads will be proposed to replace the dichotomization of triads used by Holland and Leinhardt. The new classification, which is based on the amount of transitivity and intransitivity in each triad, will predict the relative frequency of the 16 triad types. It will also allow for the reclassification of the 2-1-0 triad as permissible. The Davis pool of 742 sociograms, as well as the new data collected, will be used to test this new classification of triads.

Extension of the Model

A second weakness of the transitivity model lies in its being limited, in its present formulation, to an analysis of cliques and inter-clique structure. The model can determine the existence of cliques in a group and ranking of these cliques to form a hierarchy, but it cannot detect a ranking order within cliques. For this reason the model is under-developed. It omits one of the fundamental properties of social structure, intra-clique hierarchy, while at the same time, ignoring some of the information collected about groups which may be used to investigate within-clique ranking.

If the model were able to detect an intra-clique hierarchy, one could differentiate between cliques which have a strong status system in which there is considerable social distance between the most chosen and the least chosen members and cliques in which status is more evenly distributed. Type of within-clique hierarchy could then be related to other aspects of social structure, such as the rank of that clique in the total group, the number of cliques and hierarchies of cliques that exist in the group and the shapes of the pyramids of cliques. While social science literature contains descriptive studies of the differential status of clique members, there are, as yet, no studies of the relationship between the existence of a status hierarchy based on friendship within a group and other structural properties of the group. Extending the transitivity model by enabling it to detect within-clique ranking would open the door to studies of this type. In the present research a method of extending the model to include intra-clique hierarchy by use of the mutual choices obtained from ranked sociometric data will be developed.

Alteration of Data Collection Techniques

Rigorous empirical testing of the transitivity model is extremely important at this stage of its development. The original model, as formulated by Holland and Leinhardt, has received only minimal testing and that on data of poor quality. The data bank used was gathered by Davis and Leinhardt and includes sociograms which were collected by traditional sociometric methods. It will be argued that these methods are subject to severe criticism when used to test structural models because they produce data which contain structural bias and measurement error.

In addition, Davis and Leinhardt's data came from sociometric tests which asked a variety of questions. They assumed that the responses to each of these questions revealed the same structure, namely, the sentiment structure of the group. In order to test this assumption the author performed a pilot study on four student groups. Each group of children was asked the following four sociometric questions: who are your three best friends, who would you prefer to have as your three best friends, which three students would you like to select you as their best friend, which three students would you like to serve with you on a committee. The responses to these questions, three of which were directly related to friendship, contained enough variation to seriously challenge Davis and Leinhardt's assumption.

These criticisms of the methodological techniques used to gather the Davis-Leinhardt data point to the difficulty involved in collecting data which does not contain a bias in favor of or against the model. On the one hand, any restriction on the number of responses to the sociometric question operates, to some degree at least, against the model. On the other hand, ranked data either result in all mutual choices, in which case they cannot be used to test the model, or raise the difficult question of what cut-off point to use to determine mutual, asymmetric and null choices. Since Davis and Leinhardt did not use ranked data, none of their data was bias free. In a very real sense then, one can say that the transitivity model has not yet been tested. A data collection procedure will be proposed and utilized in this study which will avoid the criticisms leveled against the Davis and Leinhardt data and which can be used to provide a valid test of the transitivity model and the improved model.

Significance of the Study

Certain characteristics of traditional sociometric studies prevent the authors from accomplishing their intended goal, namely, the mapping of group structure. Specifically, an emphasis on the individual, the assumption that a mono-clique is the ideal sentiment structure, and a restriction to visual analysis have limited sociometric studies to investigations of the correlates of individual behavior in groups. Social structure is systemic and generalizable. It involves individuals in linkages beyond the binary level which are the result of processes acting upon all group members. The complexity of social structure requires a more sophisticated methodology for analysis than traditionally has been employed.

The partial order model of sentiment structure and the statistical techniques developed to test it provide a device for rigorous investigation of the structure of a group's social system. The model has the power to go beyond the individualistic perspective and to reveal basic laws which constrain group behavior regardless of the personalities involved. It can reveal patterns of regularity in friendship relations, and these observed patterns, according to Nadel, are social structure. The organizing principle of human behavior in small-scale sentiment groups which the model suggests is transitivity. The partial order model provides a method of testing this principle and the structure which results from it, namely, hierarchies of ranked clusters of cliques.

The main contribution of this study is methodological. The proposed improvement of the model should increase both its utility and its potential. Modifying the model by providing a new ordering of triads should offer new insights into the psychological mechanisms which constrain sentiment relations. Extending the model to structure within cliques should provide a means of testing the effect of differential adherence to a common normative system and should give new meaning to the categories of star, isolate, fringer, and so forth. The new data collection technique will insure greater accuracy in testing the model.

The theoretical and practical significance of this study can be measured by the importance of the concept of social structure to educators and to sociologists. Support for the model will reflect the necessity of perceiving the classroom as a social system, that is, an ongoing set of interrelated processes whose different components mutually fit and adapt to one another in a logically consistent fashion. It will suggest that cliques and hierarchies are fundamental to classroom groups and that any attempt to improve social relations must be made with this awareness. In addition, the model provides a sophisticated tool to assist in investigating the effects of social structure on the learning process. Knowledge gained from studies of this type will provide insight into such phenomena as the effect of a more flexible school organization on learning. Similar studies investigating the relationship between relevant independent and dependent variables and social structure may have great impact on decision-making in the schools of the future.

The implications of the study for the field of sociology should be equally great. The large majority of small group studies have been performed in social psychology laboratories in controlled and often contrived settings. The model provides a tool which will enable sociologists to study group dynamics and social structure in a natural setting and on a larger scale. The insight which the model affords into fundamental laws of social organization, whether it be the organization of sentiments, attitudes, cognitions or behavior, is a valuable addition to the study of small groups.

CHAPTER II

Data Collection Technique and Sample

The purpose of Chapter II is threefold: (1) to demonstrate the inadequacy of traditional methods of collecting sociometric data for testing structural models; (2) to introduce a new data collection technique not susceptible to the weaknesses of the former methods; and (3) to describe data collected by this method to test the transitivity model.

Inadequacy of Traditional Sociometric Data Collection Techniques

There are several types of sociometric tests in the literature (Coombs, 1964). The most popular of these, because of ease of administration, is the fixed-choice method, in which each group member is required to choose a set number of other group members according to a criterion such as friendship. Another commonly used method is the free choice procedure, which is the same as the fixed-choice method, except that there are no imposed limitations on the number of choices each group member can make. A third method is the rank order, which obtains from each group member a complete ranking of all the other members of his group. Paired comparisons, a technique similar to ranking, requires the subject to compare each possible pair of members, excluding himself, and to indicate a preference for one of the two persons in each pair. There are also sociometric techniques which combine features of the above methods. One example is the partial ranking procedure, which is comparable to the fixed-choice method except that the designated number of choices are ordered.

Sociometric data collected by these methods are subject to two weaknesses: measurement error and structural bias. Measurement error is the difference between the true sentiment structure of the group and the structure of responses given on a sociometric test. The true sentiment structure of the group is the actual pattern or arrangement of the sentiment relations of the group members. Since patterns of affect are not directly observable, it is necessary to measure them by a sociometric test. However, the sociometric responses of a group on a test often deviate from the true structure. The amount of measurement error, or disparity between true and measured sentiment relations, is determined by restrictions imposed on the subjects' choices by the testing procedure and by physical and psychological factors affecting the subjects during the testing.

Measurement error is extremely likely in sociometric data collected by both the fixed and free choice methods. The error in fixed-choice data can be illustrated by considering the three-choice test in which each subject is asked to choose three friends (preferred according to some criterion) from among the group members. In responding to the question, the subject finds himself in either of three situations: (a) he likes exactly three persons in the group and can list all three on the test, (b) he likes more than three persons and is forced to eliminate some of them in responding to the sociometric questions, or (c) he likes fewer than three persons and is forced to choose from outside his circle of friends to satisfy the requirements of the sociometric test. Only in the first situation does the sociometric question detect the true friendship relations of the subject. Since it is highly improbable that all the group members will have exactly three friends, the three-choice constraint is likely to force some of the subjects to give responses which do not match their true preferences. The structure of these responses may deviate quite drastically from the true structure of the group. A similar situation will exist in every fixed-choice test regardless of the number of choices allowed.

In a free-choice test, measurement error stems from both psychological constraints and an "expansion bias". Bjerstedt (Bjerstedt, 1955) found that most subjects give only three or four names on a free-choice test. Holland and Leinhardt (Holland and Leinhardt, 1969) suggest that this is evidence of a "response norm". A subject may feel constrained, consciously or unconsciously, to list a certain number of names. The response pattern could result from the instructions of a test administrator who hints that a certain number of choices is appropriate, from the subject's having taken fixed-choice sociometric tests previously, or from his belief that listing as many or as few persons as he considers friends is unacceptable. In addition, free choice data are subject to an "expansion bias" which results from a subject's forgetting to list one or more persons who actually are his friends. Both psychological constraints and an "expansion bias" mask the true structure of the group.

Measurement error is less likely in tests which employ ranking and paired comparison techniques. However, these techniques offer no way of distinguishing mutual, asymmetric and null relations. They cannot be used without modification to test structural models.

The second weakness of traditional sociometric methods is structural bias which is evident when structural models are being tested. Structural bias occurs when the sociometric method imposes a constraint on choices which forces responses in favor of or against the model. These biases are most likely to appear in the fixed-choice method, and are most severe when the choices are limited to a small number of responses. The biases can be illustrated by considering a one-choice and a three-choice test.

When the sociometric response is restricted to one choice, it is impossible to detect any of the following triads: 0-3-0T, 1-2-0U, 1-2-0D, 3-0-0, 1-1-1U, 2-1-0, 1-2-0C and 2-0-1. These triads can be obtained only if at least one member of the triad chooses more than one person. Since the transitivity principle always involves two choices by one member of a triad, restriction to one choice eliminates all the transitive triads. Four intransitive triads are eliminated for the same reason, leaving only the vacuously transitive and three intransitive triads as possible occurrences. It is clearly impossible for single-choice sociomatrices in which transitivity can never occur to support a transitivity model.

Allowing three responses to the sociometric question creates two biases. First, the transitivity model demands that mutual choice relations exist among all members of a clique. Under the three choice limitation, the largest clique that can be obtained has only four members; a larger clique could be detected only if more choices were allowed. If a larger clique did exist in the group, its members would not be able to identify all their friends and would be forced to select three from among them. This would increase the likelihood of obtaining intransitive triads and would mask the support which the data should provide for the model. Moreover, the arbitrary selection of three friends from within the clique even makes it unlikely that the model will be able to detect four-man subsets of the larger clique, because no four members of the clique may choose the necessary set of friends. For example, to identify a four -member subset of a six-member clique, all four members of the subset must simultaneously choose one another and simultaneously exclude the remaining two members of the larger clique. This simultaneous exclusion within a clique is highly unlikely. Consequently, restriction of the size of cliques hides existent transitive triads and forces non-existent intransitive ones.

The second bias created by the three-choice answer is less obvious. According to the transitivity model, a group member must choose every member in every clique above him in the same hierarchy. If there are more than three levels in the hierarchy, the choice restrictions make this impossible because the subject has only three choices at his disposal. The respondents are not given the freedom to express the transitivity which might exist, resulting in forced intransitive triads and hiding support for the model.

The free choice technique can also yield data which contain structural biases. Whenever the "response norm" places constraints on the number of responses to a test, the free-choice procedure is vulnerable to the same biases described for the fixed-choice method.

The above arguments demonstrate that the traditional methods of collecting sociometric data are susceptible to measurement error and structural bias. These weaknesses are serious enough to disqualify the methods as valid data collection techniques for a test of the transitivity model. As a consequence, an alternate data collection technique, not subject to the same weaknesses, is needed. The author has developed a method of collecting sociometric data which has the advantage of reducing measurement error and eliminating structural biases. A description of this method follows.

The Data Collection Technique

The sociometric criterion selected for the test of the transitivity model was friendship. A friend was defined as someone the subject likes. By offering a single conceptual base for response this definition avoids conceptual confusion often found in sociometric data.

According to the new technique, subjects are requested to divide the group members into three categories — "best friends", "friends", and "everyone else". In filling each category the respondents may list as many or as few members as they desire.[5] If they choose, they may list everyone in just one or two categories, and leave the other(s) empty. Ultimately, each respondent must put every group member, except himself, in one of the three categories. Following this, the subjects are asked to rank the persons they have listed as "best friends", designating the person they like most, as one, their second best friend, as two, and so forth. Ties are allowed; in fact, if they choose, the subjects may tie all of their best friends by giving them all the same rank. The ranking process is repeated for the category of "friend". The subjects rank in the third category only if they experience any degree of liking for the persons listed there. If some people remain unranked in this category, the test administrator ties them for last place. This process yields a rank order of the whole group by each member as well as a three category classification.

Mutual, asymmetric and null relations are determined by using the subjects' cut-off points for best friends. When two subjects list each other as best friends, the choice relation is defined as mutual. When a subject classifies a group member as best friend and the choice is reciprocated in either of the other two categories, the relation is asymmetrical. The relation is defined as null when neither subject classifies the other as best friend. In Chapter VII the use of the ranking within each category will be illustrated; in subsequent research the definition of mutual relations will be extended to include friend for an alternate test of the transitivity model.

This sociometric technique has several advantages over commonly used methods. The greatest of these is that it avoids forced choices by allowing each subject to determine his own cut-off point for each category. The subject may list as many best friends and as many friends as he wishes. This eliminates the structural biases present in the fixed-choice method and reduces measurement error due to discrepancies between a subject's actual number of friends and choices allowed.

The new procedure also avoids the major weaknesses in the free-choice method by overcoming the problem of an "expansion bias" and a "response norm." The requirement to list everyone in the group brings into awareness some who would be forgotten otherwise and increases the likelihood that such persons are classed as friends. It also reduces the psychological influences which constrain the number of choices made. the method prevents the administrator from suggesting overtly or covertly that a certain number of choices is appropriate. Previous conditioning by fixed-choice tests cannot affect the number of responses because the subject must categorize every person in the group. Finally, the subject's fear that it is unacceptable to list a certain number of persons in one category is eliminated because the test instructions emphasize individual cut-off points.

Allowing ties gives the technique the advantage of being realistic for the subjects. For some respondents it is extremely difficult, if not impossible, to differentiate between friends on the basis of the amount of affect they experience for them. Some subjects may be able to make this distinction for certain group members but not for others. The paired comparison technique as well as the ranking partial ranking methods assume that it is possible for the subjects to distinguish between their feelings for each group member. The new method avoids this assumption and allows for individual differences in ability to rank group members.

Another strong feature of the method is that it deals adequately with negative feelings. Many persons who have administered sociometric tests in schools have encountered the reluctance of parents and teachers to having an experimenter ask the children whom they dislike, or who their enemies are. They argue that the question causes the subjects to focus on negative feelings when these feelings are better ignored. Probing negative choices may also cause children who do not experience negative feelings to generate them by the power of suggestion. While this opposition is understandable, at the same time children responding to a free-choice or rank order sociometric test frequently do ask what to do with the names of group members they dislike. The new technique enables each subject to list, in the category of "everyone else", the group members they dislike or about whom they are indifferent, without having to articulate the negative feeling. When asked to rank in the last category only to the extent that it is meaningful, they can simply eliminate from the ranking anyone toward whom they hold no positive affect without having to dwell on their real feelings toward that person. This method of handling negative feelings is viable because the data are being collected to test a model of the positive sentiment structure of a group.

By reducing structural biases and measurement error, the new data collection technique provides a method of obtaining high quality sociometric data. The technique is particularly appropriate for gathering data to test structural models. This kind of data makes a rigorous test of the transitivity model possible.

The Data

Since transitivity of sentiment is hypothesized for all friendship groups, the only requirement for a sample to test the transitivity model is that the groups have a natural boundary for friendship choices. To meet this condition, a sample of children's groups was chosen from small schools which had only one class per grade level or had self-contained rather than departmentalized classes. Since many schools satisfy this requirement, socio-economic characteristics became secondary criteria for selection. Finally, when a wide range of socio-economic characteristics were represented, ease of accessibility and location became considerations. Using these criteria, fourteen schools in New York and Illinois were selected. Two of these schools were located in New York City, ten on eastern Long Island, one in Chicago and one in a suburb of Chicago.

Whenever possible, all the classes on the sixth, seventh and eighth grade levels in each of these schools were used. Some classes had to be eliminated because of the large number of absentees on the day the test was administered. The final sample included fifty-one groups with the following grade distribution: seventeen sixth grades, sixteen seventh grades, sixteen eighth grades, one fifth-sixth and one seventh-eighth grade combination. Forty-five classes contained both boys and girls; one sixth, one seventh and one eighth grade contained only boys and one of each of these grades contained only girls. The distribution of the groups by size is given in Table 1.

TABLE 1

Frequency Distribution of Groups According to Number of Students.

Number of Students	Frequency of Groups
10–14	4
15–19	14
20–24	16
25–29	12
30–34	5

Sociometric data were gathered by the present author from each of these groups using the data collection procedure described. When a member of a class was absent on the day the test was administered, arrangements were made with the teacher and principal to have the child take the test under the teacher's supervision the next time he was in school. The teachers cooperated in this effort in every case with the result that complete data were obtained from all fifty-one groups. These sociograms became the data pool on which the transitivity and the modified models were subsequently tested.

In Chapter II it is argued that traditional methods of collecting sociometric data are inadequate for testing structural models. A new technique for gathering sociometric data is developed which avoids structural biases and reduces measurement error. The technique is used to gather a pool of fifty-one sociograms for a test of the transitivity model.

CHAPTER III

Measures of Structure

Holland and Leinhardt (Holland and Leinhardt, 1970) test the transitivity model by measuring the tendency of a given directed graph (sociogram) to deviate from a random model in the direction of the transitivity model. The structural index τ which they use for this purpose will be described in the present chapter. Since τ is a test statistic and not a measure of relationship, its usefulness as an index of structure is limited. An alternate index $\hat{T}$ will be defined to measure approximation to the transitivity model. Finally, the index $\hat{T}_-$ will be formulated as a measure of comparison.

The Structural Index τ

A sociogram which contains no intransitive triads possesses the structure of hierarchies of ranked clusters of cliques depicted by the transitivity model. However, the appearance of a sociogram with this property is highly unlikely. Consequently, a structural index is needed to approximate the fit of empirical data to the deterministic model. The index τ is derived for this purpose.

Let T equal the total number of intransitive triads in a given sociogram. When T = 0, the sociogram is transitive and when T is small, the sociogram exhibits a strong tendency toward transitivity. The baseline for comparison is a sociogram obtained by randomly distributing the given number of mutual, asymmetric and null choice relations among the g members of the group. An empirical sociogram which contains about as many intransitive triads as this random graph shows little evidence of a tendency toward transitivity. A sociogram which contains significantly fewer intransitive triads than predicted by chance approximates the structure depicted by the transitivity model.

Let μ_T be the mean number of intransitive triads in a sociogram under the null hypothesis that the sociometric choices are randomly distributed and let σ_T be the standard deviation of T. The index τ is defined as follows:

$$\tau = \frac{T - \mu_T}{\sigma_T} \tag{1}$$

τ has the mean zero and variance one under the null hypothesis. The distribution of the index is approximately normal as demonstrated by Holland and Leinhardt in a simulation study. A one-sided test of the null hypothesis determines whether a sociogram deviates significantly from randomness in the direction of the deterministic model.

The formulas which Holland and Leinhardt derived for finding the mean and variance of T in the random model are outlined here for purposes of clarification and reference. Let the intransitive triad types 0-2-1C, 0-3-0C, 1-1-1D, 1-1-1U, 1-2-0C, and 2-0-1 be called type 1, type 2, . . ., type 6 respectively. Let T_i be the number of triads of type i that appear in a given sociogram. Then T, the total number of intransitive triads, is given by

$$T = T_1 + T_2 + \ldots + T_6 \tag{2}$$

From (2) and standard formulas one obtains

$$\mu_T = \sum_i E(T_i) \text{ and} \tag{3}$$

$$\sigma_T^2 = \sum_i \text{Var}(T_i) + 2 \sum_{i<j} \text{Cov}(T_i, T_j) \tag{4}$$

In order to calculate μ_T and σ_T^2 it is sufficient to compute $E(T_i)$, $\text{Var}(T_i)$ and $\text{Cov}(T_i, T_j)$. Theorem 4 expresses these quantities in terms of certain probabilities which may be computed from the random model.

Theorem 4: If T is the number of triads of type i in a random graph on g points then

(a) $E(T_i) = \binom{g}{3} p(i)$

(b) $Var(T_i) = \binom{g}{3} p(i) [1 - p(i)] + 3(g - 3)$

$\binom{g}{3} [p_2(i, i) - p_0(i, i)]$

$+ 3 \binom{g-3}{2} \binom{g}{3} [p(i, i) - p_0(i, i)]$

$+ \binom{g}{3}^{(2)} [p_0(i, i) - p_2(i)]$

(c) $Cov(T_i, T_j) = - \binom{g}{3} p(i) p(j) + 3(g - 3) \binom{g}{3}$

$[p_2(i, j) - p_0(i, j)$

$+ 3 \binom{g-3}{2} \binom{g}{3} [p_i(i, j) - p_0$

$(i, j)]$

$+ \binom{g}{3}^{(2)} [p_0(i, j) - p(i) p(j)]$

Since theorem 4 does not depend on a particular random model, any model which does not utilize the labels of the points can be employed to calculate τ.[6]

τ will be used in Chapter IV of the present study to test the fit of the transitivity model and alternate weighted models on sentiment based sociometric data and in Chapter VIII to test the models on competence based data. In Chapter VII the index will be employed to test the transitivity model on sentiment data in cliques.

Limitations of τ

The structural index τ contains three weaknesses when used as a measure of the fit of the transitivity model. First, as a test statistic, τ cannot be used to measure strength of relationship. Secondly, a test of the significance of τ is extremely difficult when g is small. Finally, the validity of τ as an index of structure depends on the appropriateness of the random model on which it is based.

Using a test statistic like τ to measure the deviation of a socio-

33

gram from a random model in the direction of a graph-theoretic model reveals little about how closely the ːɔciogram approximates the deterministic model. On the one hand, a sociogram may differ significantly from randomness but have a poor fit to the deterministic model. On the other hand, a sociogram which possesses the exact structure of the deterministic model may not deviate significantly as much from the random model. Two examples will illustrate these points.

Consider a sociogram in which $g = 18$, $M = 30$, $A = 39$ and $N = 84$. A graph with these characteristics attains maximum deviation from randomness or perfect structure when $\tau = -21.33$. If the given sociogram has a τ-value of -7.11, the graph possesses significant deviation from randomness ($p < 0.01$). However, the graph attains only 33% of the possible deviation, implying that the structure of the graph is not very close to the structure of the deterministic model. In contrast, a sociogram in which $g = 5$, $M = 6$, $A = 4$ and $N = 0$ has a maximum τ value of -2.51. A sociogram with these characteristics cannot deviate from randomness to the same extent as the sociogram in the previous example, regardless of how close it may be to the deterministic model. These examples show that the value of τ obtained from a graph reveals little about the amount of structure actually present in the graph.

Since τ does not measure approximation to the transitivity model, the index cannot be used to compare the structure of two groups or the fit of two models. Comparison between two groups on a structural basis involves determining which group actually possesses more structure. Similarly, testing the fit of two models necessitates discovering which model actually receives more support in a sociogram. By merely measuring deviation from a random model, τ cannot determine the amount of structure possessed by a graph and consequently, cannot be used for these comparisons.

The second weakness of τ is that the feasibility of using the index for tests of significance is dependent on τ's approximation to the normal distribution. For a given sociogram the maximum number of values which can assume is one more than the number of triads in the graph. When g is large the number of possible values of τ is large and the distribution of τ closely approximates the continuous standard normal distribution. However, when $g \leqslant 5$, τ can take on at most 11 values. In these cases, it is possible

TABLE 2

Comparison of Exact and Normal Distribution of τ (g = 5, M = 6, A = 4, N = 0).

Number of Intransitive Triads	τ Values	Exact Distribution	Normal Distribution
10	−4.87	0.003	0.000+
9	−4.10	0.000	0.000+
8	−3.37	0.000	0.001
7	−2.56	0.012	0.009
6	−1.89	0.054	0.052
5	−1.16	0.107	0.147
4	−0.43	0.268	0.261
3	+ 0.31	0.357	0.272
2	+ 1.04	0.116	0.177
1	+ 1.79	0.089	0.064
0	+ 2.51	0.006	0.015

that the normal distribution may not adequately represent the distribution of τ.

To investigate this possibility, the exact distribution of τ was found for a sociogram in which g = 5, M = 6, A = 4 and N= 0.[6a] In Table 2 the exact probabilities are compared to the probabilities obtained from the normal curve. The results show that the exact distribution approximates the normal distribution in the neighborhood of the mean but deviates seriously at the ends. The normal probabilities for the critical τ values of −2.56, +1.79 and +2.51 differ from the exact probabilities by a factor of about 1.5. Of these three values, +2.51 is the only one for which the normal probability is a conservative estimate of the exact probability. Consequently, the risk of error in rejecting the null hypothesis is twice what the normal curve indicates for three critical values. The example illustrates that the normal distribution may be a poor approximation to the exact distribution of τ when g $\leqslant$ 5. If g > 5 but M and A are small, the number of possible values of τ is also small and the distribution may deviate again from normal. Since the exact distribution of τ for a given sociogram is extremely difficult to obtain, tests of the significance of τ are practically impossible for these cases.

The third limitation of τ is that its validity as a measure of the fit of a structural model is determined by the choice of a random distribution. Different random models yield different values of τ which may or may not be monotonically related. Holland and Leinhardt obtained their random distribution by fixing the number of mutual, asymmetric and null relations and assigning these randomly throughout the group. They suggest that a more appropriate model would fix choices made, choices received and mutual choices. However, the mathematical results needed to obtain the chance distribution under these constraints are not yet available. As a consequence, τ is based on a random model which is not totally suitable for sentiment choices.

The Structural Index $\hat{T}$

In order to obtain a structural index not subject to the weakness of τ, $\hat{T}$ is defined. Let $\hat{T}$ be given by (5)

$$\hat{T} = \frac{T - T_{min}}{T_{max} - T_{min}} = \frac{T}{T_{max}} \tag{5}$$

where T is the number of intransitive triads in a given sociogram and T_{min} and T_{max} respectively are the minimum and maximum number of intransitive triads possible in that sociogram. Since a sociogram need not contain any intransitive triads, $T_{min} = 0$. $\hat{T}$ is a linear function of T which ranges between 0 and +1. When $\hat{T} = 0$, the graph has the exact structure of the deterministic model and when $\hat{T} = +1$ the pattern of triads cannot deviate any further from the deterministic structure.

The value of T_{max} is constrained by characteristics of the sociogram. The number of choices made, choices received and mutual choices seem to be relevant properties to consider when obtaining T_{max}. To calculate T_{max} after the constraints have been assigned requires either obtaining the exact distribution of τ for each sociogram or devising an algorithm which would yield T_{max} for each graph.

$\hat{T}$ is an appropriate index of structure for comparative tests because it is a measure of relationship. In addition, when $\hat{T}$ is standardized, it can be used for statistical tests. However, the results needed to use $\hat{T}$, namely, the value of T_{max} calculated by either of the methods suggested, the values of $\mu_{\hat{T}}$ and $\sigma_{\hat{T}}$ and the distribution of $\hat{T}$, are not available at the present time. Consequently, $\hat{T}$ merely is presented in this study as the ideal index of structure for tests of the transitivity model.

The Structural Indices $\hat{T}_+$ and $\hat{T}_-$

While $\hat{T}$ cannot be obtained in the present study, the nature of the data makes the use of an alternate split-level index possible. Consider the measures $\hat{T}_+$ and $\hat{T}_-$ defined as follows:

$$\text{if } T > \mu_T, \quad \hat{T}_+ = \frac{T - \mu_T}{T_{max} - \mu_T}$$

$$\text{if } T \leqslant \mu_T, \quad \hat{T}_- = \frac{\mu_T - T}{\mu_T + T_{min}} = 1 - \frac{T}{\mu_T} \tag{6}$$

Both $\hat{T}_+$ and $\hat{T}_-$ range between 0 and +1. Since the hypothesis of transitivity suggests that $T < \mu_T$ for all sociograms depicting sentiment choices, $\hat{T}_-$ is an appropriate measure of structure in sentiment data.

Uses of $\hat{T}_-$

The structural index $\hat{T}_-$ is a descriptive measure of the approximation of a sociogram to the transitivity model. $\hat{T}_-$ is useful for three kinds of analyses: (1) to measure the fit of the transitivity model to sociometric data, (2) to compare the fit of the transitivity model in different groups, and (3) to determine the relative success of different structural models.

Since $\hat{T}_-$ is a direct measure of structure, it can be used as a descriptive index of the fit of the transitivity model. The index can be employed regardless of the size of the group or the number of mutual, asymmetric or null relations contained in the graph. In contrast, τ does not measure approximation to the deterministic model and cannot be used when g is small.

$\hat{T}_-$ can also be used to compare the fit of the transitivity model in different groups and to determine the success of different models. If G_1 and G_2 are two groups for which $\hat{T}_{-1} < \hat{T}_{-2}$ the transitivity model fits G_2 better than G_1 because G_2 possesses more of the structure defined by the transitivity model than G_1. Similarly, if M_1 and M_2 are two graph-theoretic models of structure, for example, the unweighted transitivity model and a weighted version of the model, and $\hat{T}_{-1} < \hat{T}_{-2}$ then M_2 obtains a better fit to the data. By making these two kinds of analyses possible, $\hat{T}_-$ facilitates several types of structural studies and permits modified versions of the transitivity model to be tested.

$\hat{T}_-$ contains one weakness also found in τ, namely, its dependency on the appropriateness of a random model. If the random model used to obtain $\hat{T}_-$ is unsuitable for sociometric choices, then $\hat{T}_-$ is meaningless as a structural measure. However, $\hat{T}_-$ is based on the random model employed by Holland and Leinhardt which closely approximates an ideal random model. Consequently, there is reason to believe that $\hat{T}_-$ is a valid measure of structure.

$\hat{T}_-$ will be used in Chapter VI to compare the fit of the transitivity model and alternate weighted models in data from the sample of 51 groups. In Chapter VII the index will be employed as a descriptive measure of the fit of the transitivity model in groups for which τ is not normally distributed. Finally, in Chapter VIII $\hat{T}_-$ will be used to compare the fit of the transitivity model in sentiment data to its success in competence based sociometric data.

In Chapter III the structural index τ, formulated by Holland and Leinhardt, is presented as a measure of the deviation of a sociogram from a random model in the direction of the transitivity model. The index $\hat{T}$ is defined as a measure of relationship which, when standardized, measures deviation from the deterministic model. $\hat{T}_-$ is proposed as a suitable descriptive measure of relationship for sentiment data. Since τ cannot determine the amount of structure in a group, $\hat{T}$ is a more suitable index of structure for tests of the transitivity model while $\hat{T}_-$ is useful for structural comparisons.

A rigorous study of sentiment is possible only when appropriate indices of structure are formulated and the conditions for their use determined. The indices defined in Chapter III allow tests of the transitivity model and comparison between the structure of different groups and the fit of different models. Consequently, these indices facilitate important aspects of the study of sentiment relations.

CHAPTER IV

Test of the Transitivity Model

Prior to the present research, the only data on which the transitivity model had been tested were a pool of 917 sociograms collected by Davis and Leinhardt to test the ranked clusters model (Davis and Leinhardt, 1972). In the present chapter it will be argued that these data contain structural biases and measurement error which make them inappropriate for a test of the model. The first rigorous test of the transitivity model on data collected specifically for this purpose will be presented. The results will provide a test of the hypothesis that sentiment relations tend to be transitive and that the structure of sentiment choices in friendship groups is hierarchies of ranked clusters of cliques. A comparison will be made between the success of the model in the Davis-Leinhardt data pool and in the new sample.

Critique of the Davis-Leinhardt Data Pool

In collecting their sociomatrices, Davis and Leinhardt imposed no *a priori* standards of quality or content on them; their goal was simply to collect as large a data pool as possible to subject to secondary analysis. The sources of their data included journal articles, yearbooks, pamphlets, unpublished theses and raw data from individual investigators. The majority of the groups were student groups, the others included adult work groups, military units and neighborhood groups. Davis and Leinhardt tested the ranked clusters model on a sample of 60 sociograms from this data pool and later Holland and Leinhardt tested the transitivity model on all the sociograms in the data bank.

The use of the Davis-Leinhardt data to test a structural model can be criticized for several reasons. In the first place, the quality of their data pool is seriously weakened by the large number of fixed-choice sociograms it contains. Three hundred and eighty-four sociomatrices (42%) are from fixed-choice tests, most of which allowed only one or three choices. These data are susceptible to the severe biases against the transitivity model described in Chapter II.

A second weakness in the data bank stems from the large number of free-choice tests. Three hundred and thirty-five groups (37%) had been tested by the free choice method. These sociograms are vulnerable to an "expansion bias" which occurs when a respondent forgets to list some of his friends. In addition, assuming that some of the subjects had taken fixed-choice tests before which is probable considering the number of children's school groups in the sample, the sociograms could be biased by a "response norm". As a result, it is very likely that the free-choice sociograms contain measurement error which masks the underlying structure of the groups.

Another criticism of Davis and Leinhardt's data is that the sociomatrices came from tests which asked different sociometric questions. The questions touched various conceptual bases such as power, status, competence and interpersonal attraction. In Chapter VIII it will be demonstrated that pooling matrices from different sociometric questions results in structural confusion which hides support for a sentiment model.

Since the Davis-Leinhardt data contain these weaknesses, the test of the transitivity model on these data loses some of its validity. The quality of the data makes it inappropriate to draw conclusions from their results about a similarity between the model's theoretical structure and the structure of sentiment relations. A more rigorous test of the model using data of higher quality is needed.

Test of the Transitivity Model on the Sample of 51 Groups

The data obtained from the sample of 51 groups were collected by the method described in Chapter II. In responding to the socio-metric questions the subjects were allowed to choose their own cut-off points for the categories of "best friends" and "friends". The set of "best friends" will be used in the test of the model. Since SOCPAC 1 contains a de-ranking procedure which allows analysis of data up to a fixed choice level, the program is particu-larly amenable to data in this form. A minor modification in the program allows a sequential analysis on these data, first analyzing all first choices, then adding second choices for all subjects who have them and analyzing the first and second choices together, then adding third choices, and continuing the process until each person's cut-off point is reached.

The value of τ was computed for each of the groups in the sample. Figure 4 shows a histogram of the 51 values. τ is negative in every group, indicating that each group contains fewer intran-sitive triads than predicted by chance. The distribution of τ is skewed toward the smaller values with a median τ-value of -11.0 and a mean of -11.7. τ is significant ($p < 0.01$) for every socio-gram in the sample. The null hypothesis that friendship choices are distributed randomly is rejected in every group and the alternative

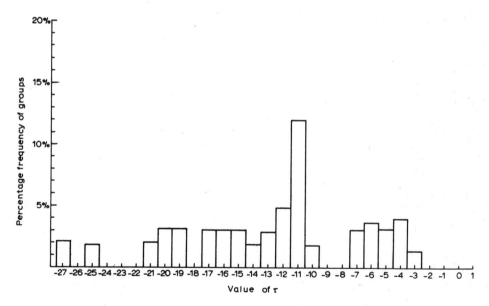

Fig. 4. Histogram of τ rounded to nearest whole number (N = 51).

hypothesis that the distribution of friendship choices approximates the structure of the transitivity model is supported. These results are strong evidence that sentiment relations tend to be transitive.

Another way of looking at the data is to examine the frequency of each intransitive triad type to determine if one particular triad is preventing the sociogram from being completely transitive. Table 3 presents the percentage of groups in the sample which have fewer of each non-permissible triad type than the random model predicts. As can be seen from the table, the 0-2-1C, 1-1-1D, 1-1-1U, 2-0-1 and 1-2-0C triads lend considerable support to the model in nearly all of the matrices. The 0-3-0C triad deprives the model of support in more than half of the matrices because its deviation from randomness fails to achieve significance. The 2-1-0 triad is even less successful with only 8% of the matrices having fewer 2-1-0 triads than predicted by chance. These results illustrate that the transitivity model's predictions of triad frequency are correct for five of the seven triads. The failure of the 0-3-0C

TABLE 3

Percentage of Sociomatrices Having Significantly Fewer of Each Intransitive Triad Type Than Predicted by Chance ($N = 51$).

Intransitive Triad Type	$p < 0.05$	$p < 0.01$
0-2-1C	84%	73%
1-1-1D	96	73
1-1-1U	76	63
0-3-0C[a]	35	29
2-0-1	98	98
1-2-0C	49	41
2-1-0	8	8

[a] In 12 sociomatrices, the expected value of the 0-3-0C triad is less than 1.00 and in one sociomatrix the expected value of the 1-2-0 triad is less than 1.00. If these matrices were eliminated from the analysis because they may cause irregular results, 38% of the sociomatrices would contain significantly fewer 0-3-0C triads than expected ($p < 0.05$) and 42% of the sociomatrices would contain significantly fewer 1-2-0 triads ($p < 0.05$).

and 2-1-0 triads to support the model will receive further consideration in Chapters IV and V.

Comparison of the Fit of the Transitivity Model on the Two Data Pools

A comparison can be made between the fit of the transitivity model on the Davis-Leinhardt data and on the sample of 51 groups. Although the values of the appropriate index for comparative tests, $\hat{T}_-$, are not available for the Davis-Leinhardt groups, a less rigorous comparison is possible. The expectation is that the model will obtain a better fit in the new data because they do not contain the structural biases which were found in the Davis-Leinhardt data.

The data will be analyzed first by comparing the percentage of matrices in the two data pools which have fewer of each intransitive triad type than predicted by the random model. The assumption is that the data pool which has a higher percentage of matrices with fewer intransitive triads than expected by chance contains more support for the model. This assumption is strengthened by comparing groups in the same size range.

Table 4 compares the percentage of matrices in the Davis-Leinhardt data and the sample of 51 groups which have fewer of each intransitive triad type than expected. Five of the six intransitive triads, namely 0-3-0C, 2-0-1, 0-2-1C, 1-1-1, and 1-2-0C, occur less frequently in the new data than in Davis and Leinhardt's for each size classification and for the total sample. The remaining 2-0-1 triad occurs more frequently than chance in a larger number of matrices in both sets of data. This triad is less successful in the new data since an average of only 8% of the matrices have fewer 2-1-0 triads than predicted by chance compared to 37% of the matrices in the Davis-Leinhardt pool. These results illustrate that the transitivity model receives substantially more support in the new data from all the triads except 2-1-0 which does not support the model in either data pool. The 2-1-0 triad will receive more attention in Chapter V where it will be shown that the triad is inaccurately classified as non-permissible. This in turn will explain its frequent occurrence in both sets of data.

A second way of analyzing the data is to compare the distri-

TABLE 4

Percentage of Sociomatrices With Intransitive Triad Frequencies Less Than Chance Expectation for Davis-Leinhardt Data and Hallinan Data According to Size of Group.

Intransitive Triad Type	Group Size							
	8–17		18–22		23–38		Total	
	D-L Data	Hallinan Data	D-L Data	Hallinan Data	D-L Data	Hallinan Data	D-L Data	Hallinan Data
0-3-0C	91% (203)[a]	100% (8)	91% (78)	100% (14)	92% (130)	94% (19)	91% (411)	98% (41)
2-0-1	88 (273)	100 (10)	92 (123)	100 (20)	90 (191)	100 (21)	89 (587)	100 (51)
0-2-1C	75 (303)	100 (10)	84 (129)	90 (20)	90 (198)	100 (21)	82 (630)	96 (51)
1-1-1	69 (315)	90 (10)	84 (132)	90 (20)	85 (198)	98 (21)	77 (645)	93 (51)
1-2-0C	85 (258)	90 (10)	81 (108)	85 (20)	64 (155)	86 (21)	78 (521)	86 (51)
2-1-0	52 (239)	30 (10)	42 (106)	5 (20)	19 (151)	0 (21)	39 (496)	8 (51)

[a] Number of sociomatrices with expected value of 1.000 or greater.

bution of τ in each set of data. It was pointed out in Chapter III that a comparison of the τ-values for two groups does not reveal which group has more structure, but an examination of the distribution of τ for two data pools should indicate which set of data contains more support for the model, especially when the difference between the means of the two distributions is large. Although the required τ-values for this kind of analysis are not available for the Davis-Leinhardt data, an alternate measure τ^* can be obtained for their data which permits the comparison.

In response to the present author's critique of their data (Hallinan, 1972) Holland and Leinhardt (Holland and Leinhardt, 1972) presented the τ^* values for 917 sociograms from their data pool where τ^* is a weighted index equivalent to the index τ_w derived in Chapter VI. τ^* is a more sensitive measure than τ, and ordinarily will obtain a better fit of the model to the data than the τ values. Consequently, if a comparison is made between the τ^* values of the Davis-Leinhardt data and the values of the 51 groups revealing that the transitivity model is more successful in the latter sample, the results can be interpreted as a conservative estimate of the relatively greater success of the model in the sample of 51 groups.

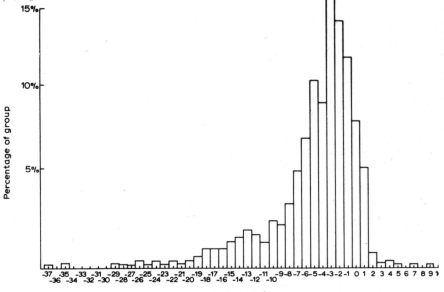

Value of τ^*

Fig. 5. Histogram is τ^* rounded to nearest whole number (N = 917).

The distribution of τ^* for the Davis-Leinhardt data is given in Figure 5. Seventy percent of the sociograms show a significant tendency toward the transitivity model. The mean of their distribution is -5.51 and the median is -4.0. Examining the same statistics in the distribution of τ for the 51 groups in Figure 4 reveals that 100% of the sociograms in the new data support the model. The distribution has a mean of -11.7 and a median of -11.0. These results indicate that the transitivity model receives much stronger support in the new data.

Discussion

The fit of the transitivity model to high quality data provides substantial support for the hypothesis that transitivity is the organizing principle of sentiment relations in friendship groups. This implies that the pattern of these relations can be depicted by hierarchies of ranked clusters of cliques. Since the model was successful in every group in a sample of sixth, seventh and eighth grade children possessing a wide variety of characteristics, one expects that it will find support in all sixth, seventh and eighth grade friendship groups. Furthermore, since Leinhardt (Leinhardt, 1968) has shown that sentiment relations among children are in the process of developing into the more stable relations found among adults, the transitivity model is expected to be even more successful in adult friendship groups.

The considerable difference in the fit of the model in the sample of 51 groups and in the Davis-Leinhardt data pool supports the contention that the Davis-Leinhardt data is biased against the model. In their response to the author's rejoinder, (Hallinan, 1972) Holland and Leinhardt (Holland and Leinhardt, 1972) acknowledge this point. They reveal the structural biases in their own data by illustrating that the average τ^* value in the data they obtained from fixed-choice tests is half the average τ^* value in their free-choice data. These results indicate that using fixed-choice data reduced support for the model by 50%. The success of the model in the new sample lends empirical support to the argument that the new data collection technique yields high quality sociometric data for tests of structural models.

Although Davis and Leinhardt's sociograms distort the underlying structure they are presumed to represent, the distortion is not sufficient to mask the general tendency toward transitivity found in their groups. The detection of transitivity in their sociograms is important because of the size and diversity of their sample. The fact that support for the transitivity model is found even in biased data, in groups which differ in age, sex and socioeconomic composition, is strong evidence that sentiment relations have a general tendency toward transitivity.

The success of the transitivity model indicates that the network of interpersonal relations in a group can be viewed as a system rather than merely as a conglomeration of individual personalities and behaviors. Social forces exist in a group to influence and constrain interdependencies among group members. These forces involve individuals in linkages beyond the binary level and create patterns of regularity in the network. The discovery of transitivity as the force which organizes sentiment relations explains the systemic and generalizable structure found in friendship groups.

CHAPTER V

Application of Balance Theory to Sentiment Relations in Triplets

The preceding chapters focused on the transitivity of sentiment relations in triads and found the transitivity model based on this concept useful in characterizing the structure of friendship relations in a group. In the present chapter the notion of transitivity will be applied to the triplets contained within each triad. The argument will be made that the number of transitive and intransitive triplets in any given triad is related to the relative frequency of that triad. If transitivity is found to be useful in predicting the frequency of the triad types, then confidence in the appropriateness of transitivity for explaining the structure of sentiment relations will be strengthened.

An understanding of the way transitivity operates in triplets could have important implications for the formulation of the transitivity model. When Holland and Leinhardt dichotomize triads into transitive and intransitive, they ignore the presence of different numbers of transitive and intransitive triplets in a triad. In testing the model they found that the intransitive 2-1-0 triad occurred too frequently to support the model but they could not explain its unpredicted behavior in terms of their theory nor could they adjust the model to the empirical reality. Examining transitivity in the triplets in a triad may yield new insights into the behavior of all the triads and in particular, the 2-1-0 triad. If this is the case, a modification of the model may be possible which would incorporate both the refined theory and the empirical findings.

Intransitive Triplets

Every triad (x, y, z) contains six triplets, namely (x, y, z), (x, z, y), (y, x, z), (y, z, x), (z, x, y) and (z, y, x). The triplets are classified as transitive, vacuously transitive or intransitive according to the definition of transitivity on (X, C). The four transitive triads contain one or more transitive triplets and no intransitive triplets. Five of the seven intransitive triads, 0-3-0C, 2-0-1, 1-1-1U, 1-1-1D and 0-2-1C contain one or more intransitive triplets and no transitive ones. The intransitive 2-1-0 and 1-2-0C triads contain both transitive and intransitive triplets while the five vacuously transitive triads contain neither transitive nor intransitive triplets.

Holland and Leinhardt's argument that imbalance explains the infrequent occurrence of intransitive triads is inaccurately applied to triads. Balance is a psychological state of an individual, not a property of a triad. Balance exists in a triad only if it is experienced by the members of the triplets in the triad. Consequently, the application of balance theory to triplets rather than triads should be theoretically more productive.

Balance theory suggests that one member of an intransitive triplet experiences a feeling of distress caused by his involvement in an unbalanced cognitive or affective relationship. In the intransitive 0-2-1C triplet (x, y, z) in Figure 6, x experiences the discomfort of inconsistency because his failure to choose z is inconsistent with his choice of y and y's choice of z. The psychological distress which x experiences is a pressure or a force which makes the triad unstable. To alleviate the discomfort, x will attempt to change the

Fig. 6. Intransitive 0-2-1 triplet.

50

bonds and to restore balance. He can do this either by replacing the negative or null bond between himself and z by a positive one or by breaking his positive bond with y. In either case, if his attempt is successful, he will eliminate the intransitivity in the triplet and restore stability. Since the intransitive triads 0-3-0C, 2-0-1, 1-1-1U, 1-1-1D and 0-2-1C contain at least one intransitive triplet and no transitive triplets, each of these triads is unstable and possesses a tendency toward change. Since instability makes the frequent appearance of these intransitive triads in a group unlikely, one expects to find these five types less frequently in empirical data than expected by chance.

An alternate interpretation of balance theory leads to the same conjecture. One can hold that an intransitive triplet, (x, y, z), is distressful to each member of the triplet. The first member, x, experiences discomfort because his relationship with the other members is inconsistent. These members also experience discomfort, either because they vicariously share x's distress or because they are aware of the tenuous nature of the triadic relationship. Their discomfort will lead them, as well as x, to attempt to modify the bonds and restore balance and stability. Again this force toward change makes the occurrence of intransitive triplets in-

TABLE 5

Frequency Distribution of Groups According to Percentage Fewer Intransitive Triads Than Expected by Chance.

Percentage Fewer Intransitive Triads Than Expected by Chance	Frequency of Groups
1— 10%	0
11— 20	2
21— 30	5
31— 40	14
41— 50	16
51— 60	6
61— 70	4
71— 80	3
81— 90	1
91—100	0

frequent. As a result, the hypothesis is that the 0-3-0C, 2-0-1, 1-1-1U, 1-1-1D, and 0-2-1 triads will occur less frequently in a sociogram than expected by chance.

The hypothesis is tested in the sample of 51 groups and in the Davis-Leinhardt data. Table 5 presents the percent fewer of these five intransitive triads in the 51 groups than expected by chance. Every group has fewer intransitive triads than predicted by the random model. The mean percent of deviation from randomness is 45% and the median of the sample is 44%. Table 3 in Chapter IV presents the Davis-Leinhardt data on 917 sociograms in the form of the percentage of matrices with fewer of each intransitive triad type than predicted by chance. The percentage of groups having fewer of the 0-3-0C, 2-0-1, 1-1-1U, 1-1-1D, and 0-2-1C triads than expected by chance is 91%, 89%, 77%, 77% and 82% respectively. Both sets of data offer strong support to the hypothesis that intransitive triads occur less frequently than expected by chance. The results indicate that these five intransitive triads are unstable because they contain intransitive triplets which possess a force toward change.

Transitive Triplets

While balance theory suggests that intransitive triads occur infrequently because they contain triplets which are psychologically distressful to the members, the theory makes the opposite prediction for transitive triads, namely, that they will appear frequently in empirical data. The basic tenet of balance theory is that the human psyche abhors inconsistency but finds satisfaction in cognitive or emotional consistency. Since a transitive triplet is balanced, the person who is involved in the two positive choice relations in the triplet derives satisfaction from the consistency of the relationship. The other two members may also experience pleasure either from their recognition of the consistency experienced by the first member or from their awareness of the stability of the relationship. The psychological experience of satisfaction which the members derive from the relationship implies that the transitive triplet is stable. This stability, as well as the tendency of intransitive triplets to become transitive, suggests that more transitive triplets will occur in empirical data than predicted by a

TABLE 6

Frequency Distribution of Groups According to Percentage More Transitive
Triads Than Expected by Chance.

Percentage More Transitive Triads Than Expected by Chance	Frequency of Groups
1– 20%	1
21– 40	1
41– 60	3
61– 80	6
81–100	10
101–120	4
121–140	7
141–160	4
161–180	2
181–200	3
over 200	8

random model. Since a transitive triad must contain at least one
transitive triplet, transitive triads are expected to occur more frequently in a sociogram than predicted by chance.

A slight modification of SOCPAC 1 allows testing of the hypothesis. The program is made to calculate the expected number
of transitive or vacuously transitive triads under the random
model, the number observed in empirical data and the percent
fewer observed than expected. Table 6 gives the results for the
sample of 51 groups. Every group contains more transitive triads
than predicted under the random hypothesis. Seven groups (14%)
contain more than three times the number expected by chance
while 30 groups (59%) have more than twice the expected number. The mean percentage of deviation from randomness in the
direction of transitivity is 138% and the median is 119%. The data
support the hypothesis and offer substantial evidence of a tendency toward transitivity in triadic relations.

Vacuously Transitive Triplets

The five vacuously transitive triads, 0-0-3, 1-0-2, 0-1-2, 0-2-1U
and 0-2-1D, contain no intransitive triplets. None of the triplets in

the triads possess the tendency to change described by balance theory which led to the prediction that the intransitive triplets would occur less frequently than by chance. On the other hand, none of the vacuously transitive triads contains transitive or balanced triplets which yield satisfaction and are stabilizing forces in a triad. Since the vacuously transitive triads contain triplets which possess neither a force toward change nor a force toward stability, the expectation is that they will have close to chance occurrence in empirical data.

Table 7 presents a test of the hypothesis. The number of vacuously transitive triads in almost half of the groups (45%) differs by less than 5% from the number predicted by chance. The mean percentage of deviation from the expected number is 6.6% and the median is 6%. Every group deviates slightly in the direction of having more vacuously transitive triads than expected

TABLE 7

Frequency Distribution of Groups According to Percentage More Vacuously Transitive Triads Than Expected by Chance.

Percentage More Vacuously Transitive Triads Than Expected by Chance	Frequency of Groups
1– 5%	23
6–10	20
11–15	7
16–20	1

rather than fewer. Since the 1-0-2 triad appears more frequently than expected in 49 of the 51 groups (98%), it is responsible for this slight bias toward transitivity. The results suggest that the 1-0-2 triad, which represents a dyadic relationship, is more stable than the other vacuously transitive triads. The behavior of this triad merits further study. The overall results lend strong support to the hypothesis that the vacuously transitive triads occur with a frequency close to chance expectation.

The 2-1-0 and 1-2-0C Triads

The frequencies of the remaining two triads, 2-1-0 and 1-2-0C, are not as easily predicted by balance theory as are the frequencies of the other 14 triads. The 2-1-0 triad possesses three transitive and one intransitive triplet while the 1-2-0C triad has one transitive and two intransitive triplets. The presence of both transitive and intransitive triplets in these triads makes predicting their frequencies problematic. Balance theory suggests that the distress caused by the intransitive triplets in the triads impels at least one member of the triplet to change the relationship in order to remove the intransitivity. On the other hand, the satisfaction derived from the transitive triplets should make the triad stable. The question becomes how these contradictory forces resolve themselves and which one dominates.

If one assumes that the forces of transitivity and intransitivity are equally strong, the combination is a simple linear function f of the number of transitive (t) and intransitive ($-i$) triplets in the triad (7).

$$f = t + i \qquad (7)$$

The function associates with each triad a signed number indicating whether transitivity or intransitivity dominates. In the 2-1-0 triad, $f = +2$ which classifies the triad as transitive; in the 1-2-0C triad, $f = -1$ making it intransitive.

A second method of combining the forces is based on the assumption that the tendency away from intransitivity has a different strength from the tendency to remain transitive. Since intransitivity is a psychologically painful state, one might expect that its negative valence is greater than the positive valence attached to the psychologically satisfying state of consistency. The combination of forces which this assumption suggests is given by (8) in which an intransitive triplet is assigned twice the weight of a transitive one.

$$g = t + 2i \qquad (8)$$

Using this function, the 2-1-0 triad yields a value of +1 and the 1-2-0C triad a value of -3, classifying the triads again as transitive and intransitive respectively.

55

Numerous other linear and curvilinear combinations of the number of transitive and intransitive triplets in these triads could be suggested. However, finding the most accurate function is not of immediate concern; this can be accomplished later by performing a regression analysis on the data. The present goal is simply to make a reasonable prediction about the frequency of each of the triads and the two functions f and g are sufficient for this purpose. Using either function, the transitivity in the 2-1-0 triad outweighs the intransitivity, leading to the prediction that the 2-1-0 triad will occur more frequently than by chance. In the 1-2-0C triad, both functions indicate that the triad contains more intransitivity than transitivity suggesting that the 1-2-0C triad will occur less frequently than by chance.

The predicted frequencies of the 1-2-0C and 2-1-0 triads can be tested in the sample of 51 groups. Table 8 gives the distribution of groups according to the percent more 2-1-0 triad which each group contains than expected by chance. Forty-seven of the 51 groups

TABLE 8

Frequency Distribution of Groups According to Percentage More 2-1-0 Triads Than Expected by Chance.

Percentage More 2-1-0 Triads Than Expected by Chance	Frequency of Groups
1– 10%	1
11– 20	5
21– 30	5
31– 40	8
41– 50	3
51– 60	4
61– 70	6
71– 80	3
81– 90	3
91–100	4
over100	5
	47[a]

[a] Four of the 51 groups contain fewer 2-1-0 triads than expected by chance with percentages of 5%, 6%, 33% and 47%.

TABLE 9

Frequency-Distribution of Groups According to Percentage Fewer 1-2-0C Triads Than Expected by Chance.

Percentage Fewer 1-2-0C Triads Than Expected by Chance	Frequency of Groups
1– 10%	5
11– 20	2
21– 30	5
31– 40	4
41– 50	6
51– 60	4
61– 70	5
71– 80	6
81– 90	1
91–100	7[a]
	45[b]

[a] Four of these seven groups contain 100% fewer 1-2-0C triads than expected by chance, that is, they contain no 1-2-0C triads.
[b] Six of the 51 groups contain more 1-2-0C triads than expected by chance with percentages of 5%, 8%, 8%, 25%, 78% and 125%.

(92%) have more 2-1-0 triads than expected. The mean percentage of deviation from the expected number for these groups is 61% and the median is 58%. Only four groups have fewer 2-1-0 triads than expected with percent deviations of 5%, 6%, 33%, and 47%. The results support the hypothesis that the 2-1-0 triad occurs more frequently than by chance.

Table 9 presents the distribution of groups based on the percent fewer 1-2-0C triads than predicted by chance. Forty-five of the 51 groups (88%) have fewer 1-2-0C triads than expected in the random model. Four groups (5%) contain 100% fewer 1-2-0C triads than expected, implying that they possess no 1-2-0C triads. The mean percentage of deviation from the expected number is 52% and the median is 57%. The six remaining groups have more 1-2-0C triads than predicted, with percentages of 5%, 8%, 8%, 25%, 78% and 125%. While the three latter groups lend no support to the hypothesis, the first three do not deviate seriously from randomness. The overall results lend strong support to the proposition that the 1-2-0C triad will appear less frequently than chance in empirical data. The success of the predicted frequencies of both 2-1-0 and 1-2-0C indicates that the methods of combining the transitive and intransitive triplets obtained by the functions f and g have empirical validity.

The Rank Ordering of Triads

The application of balance theory to triplets in a triad led to a prediction of the frequency of occurrence of the intransitive, vacuously transitive and transitive triads with respect to the random model. Further reflection on the way balance theory operates in triplets will lead to a proposition regarding the relative frequency of each of the 16 triad types.

Balance theory suggests that the presence of an intransitive triplet makes a triad unstable and its occurrence unlikely. From this one can argue that if two intransitive triplets are present in the triad, a second person experiences discomfort and a second force is present to change the nature of the triad. This makes the appearance of a triad with two intransitive triplets less likely than a triad which contains only one. Similarly, if one assumes that every member in an intransitive triplet suffers the distress from each inconsistent triplet in the triad, a second intransitive triplet increases the distress of all three members. The added effort which the members expend to change the triad makes its appearance less likely. This reasoning leads to the prediction that the more intransitive triplets contained in a triad which has no transitive triplets, the less likely is the appearance of the triad in empirical data.

A similar prediction can be made for the transitive triads. Each time a transitive triplet is added to a triad, the members of the triad are involved in greater consistency and receive more satisfaction from the relationship. The triad with the most transitive triplets is the most desirable to the members and the most stable. In triads which contain fewer transitive triplets, the members will attempt to alter the bonds in order to increase the number of transitive triplets. Therefore, one expects that the greater the number of transitive triplets in a triad which contains no intransitive triplets, the more likely is the triad to occur in empirical data.

58

The vacuously transitive triads have been found to occur close to chance frequency. Consequently, one expects that they will appear more often than intransitive triads and less often than transitive triads. Moreover, since balance theory offers no rationale for predicting differential frequency among the vacuously transitive triads, they are not expected to differ significantly among themselves in frequency.

The functions f and g allow the frequency of the 2-1-0 and 1-2-0C triads relative to the other triads to be predicted. The function f gives the 2-1-0 triad a score of +2, implying that it will occur as frequently as the transitive triads which contain two transitive triplets. The 1-2-0C triad is given a weight of −1 which suggests that its frequency is close to that of the intransitive triads which contain one intransitive triplet. When one assumes that g is the appropriate method of combining the transitive and intransitive triplets in a triad, 2-1-0 is given a weight of +1 and 1-2-0C a weight of −3. Here, their expected frequencies are comparable to triads which contain one transitive and three intransitive triplets respectively.

The above propositions imply two ranked orderings of the 16 triad types from the most intransitive to the most transitive, that is, from the least likely to occur to the most likely. The ranks can be determined by obtaining a bivariate score for each triad from the functions f and g. Table 10 presents these functional values. The magnitude of the score determines the frequency of each triad with respect to the others. The score does not locate the triads on an interval scale and no conclusions can be drawn about how much more frequently a given triad will appear.

Table 11 presents the theoretical rank orders, R_f and Rg, obtained from f and g respectively. The rankings differ only in the location of 2-1-0 and 1-2-0C. Both rankings locate the 2-1-0 triad among the triads of highest frequency whereas Holland and Leinhardt classify it as nonpermissible, implying that it will occur infrequently. The two rankings will be tested on sociometric data to determine their validity. In addition, a comparison will be made between the success of the two orderings in order to gain insight into the way the forces of transitivity and intransitivity are combined in the 2-1-0 and 1-2-0C triads.

TABLE 10

Functional Values for f and g of Number of Transitive Triplets (t) and Intransitive Triplets (i) in Each of the Sixteen Triad Types.

Triad Type	(t, i)	f = t + i	g = t + 2i
0-3-0C	(0, −3)	−3	−6
2-1-0	(0, −2)	−2	−4
1-2-0C	(1, −2)	−1	−3
1-1-1D	(0, −1)	−1	−2
1-1-1U	(0, −1)	−1	. −2
0-2-1C	(0, −1)	−1	−2
0-1-2	(0, 0)	0	0
0-0-3	(0, 0)	0	0
1-0-2	(0, 0)	0	0
0-2-1U	(0, 0)	0	0
0-2-1U	(0, 0)	0	0
0-3-0T	(1, 0)	1	1
2-1-0	(3, −1)	2	1
1-2-0D	(2, 0)	2	2
1-2-0U	(2, 0)	2	2
3-0-0	(6, 0)	6	6

TABLE 11

Theoretical Triad Rankings R_f and R_g Derived From Functions f and g: Rankings Proceed From Least Frequently Expected to Most Frequently Expected.

R_f	R_g
0-3-0C*[a]	0-3-0C*
2-0-1*	2-0-1*
1-2-0C*, 1-1-1D*, 1-1-1U*, 0-2-1C*	1-2-0C*
0-1-2, 0-0-3, 1-0-2, 0-2-1U, 0-2-1D	1-1-1D*, 1-1-1U*, 0-2-1C*
0-3-0T	0-1-2, 0-0-3, 1-0-2, 0-2-1U, 0-2-1D
2-1-0*, 1-2-0D, 1-2-0U	0-3-0T, 2-1-0*
3-0-0	1-2-0D, 1-2-0U
	3-0-0

[a] An asterisk denotes a triad which is classified as non-permissible by Holland and Leinhardt in the transitivity model.

Test of the Rank Orderings on 51 Groups

The rank orders are tested on the sample of 51 groups described in Chapter II. For each group the empirical ranking of the triads is calculated by SOCPAC 1. Since the probabilities of the occurrence of different triad types under the chance hypothesis vary greatly, a standardized statistic is ranked rather than the actual frequency. The statistic is given by (9) in which O is the observed number of a particular triad, E is the expected number in the random model, and SD is the standard deviation of the observed number. A modification of the computer program enables it to correlate

$$\frac{O - E}{SD} \tag{9}$$

the empirical ordering with the two theoretical orderings R_f and R_g. For each group the Spearman rank correlation coefficient for the theoretical and empirical ranks is calculated. The results are given in Table 12.

The correlation between each theoretical ranking and the empirical ranking achieves significance at the 0.001 level for 88% of the groups, at the 0.01 level for 8% of the groups and at the 0.05 level for the remaining 6%. The strong support which the data show for both theoretical orderings allows the rejection of the null hypothesis that the correlations were obtained by chance. The results indicate that the combination of transitive and intransitive triplets in a triad determines its relative frequency.

The ranking R_f derived from the function f yields higher correlation coefficients than R_g in 88% of the groups. The difference is shown to be statistically significant ($p < 0.01$) by the Wilcoxon matched-pairs signed-ranks test. The success of R_f implies that the tendency away from intransitivity is balanced by the tendency toward transitivity and that the balance is achieved when a triad contains an equal number of transitive and intransitive triplets.

Test of the Rank Orderings on the Davis-Leinhardt Data

In a recent article, James Davis (Davis, 1970) reported a test of the Davis-Leinhardt ranked clusters model on 742 sociomatrices from their data bank. Davis tabulated the results of the test in the

TABLE 12

Spearman Rank Correlations of Theoretical Rankings R_f and R_g with Empirical Ranking[a].

Group	R_f	R_g	Group	R_f	R_g	Group	R_f	R_g
1	0.779	0.762	18	0.600*	0.553*	35	0.658	0.648
2	0.730	0.716	19	0.803	0.830	36	0.637	0.617
3	0.786	0.750	20	0.564*	0.559**	37	0.769	0.727
4	0.854	0.836	21	0.626	0.606	38	0.801	0.793
5	0.677	0.655	22	0.726	0.719	39	0.860	0.827
6	0.766	0.749	23	0.702	0.686	40	0.837	0.829
7	0.774	0.755	24	0.798	0.784	41	0.679	0.684
8	0.591*	0.568*	25	0.833	0.853	42	0.753	0.749
9	0.815	0.773	26	0.696	0.660	43	0.757	0.750
10	0.836	0.820	27	0.683	0.661	44	0.822	0.787
11	0.587*	0.580*	28	0.644	0.620	45	0.718	0.731
12	0.747	0.746	29	0.789	0.749	46	0.768	0.750
13	0.554	0.538	30	0.889	0.859	47	0.739	0.694
14	0.791	0.759	31	0.740	0.700	48	0.723	0.713
15	0.827	0.827	32	0.798	0.786	49	0.585*	0.584*
16	0.540**	0.534**	33	0.907	0.896	50	0.453**	0.477*
17	0.613	0.586	34	0.662	0.670	51	0.760	0.756

[a] All coefficients are significant (p < 0.001) using the t test with d.f. = 14, except the coefficients marked by an asterisk. A single asterisk denotes significance at the 0.01 level and a double asterisk at the 0.05 level.

form of the percent of matrices with triad frequency less than chance expectation. This information can be used to perform an additional test of the proposed rank orders of triads. In the previous test of the rank order, the theoretical rankings were correlated with the empirical ranking in each group. The manner in which Davis presents his data makes this kind of analysis of his results impossible. However, an alternate though less rigorous kind of test can be performed by ranking the triads on the basis of the percent of matrices which have fewer of each triad type than expected by chance.

Table 13 gives the percentage of matrices in Davis' data which have fewer of each triad type than predicted by chance. The ranking derived from these data is presented in Table 14 with the theoretical rankings included for purposes of comparison. Davis reported results for only 13 triads since he did not distinguish between 1-1-1U and 1-1-1D, between 0-2-1U and 0-2-1D or between 1-2-0U and 1-2-0D. In order to make comparison with the

TABLE 13

Percentage of Matrices in Davis Data With Triad Frequency Less Than Chance Expectation.

Triad Type	Percentage of Matrices	
0-3-0C	90%	(441)[a]
2-0-1	90	(651)
0-2-1C	83	(701)
1-1-1	78	(716)
1-2-0C	75	(563)
0-1-2	42	(708)
0-0-3	41	(649)
2-1-0	37	(530)
1-0-2	37	(706)
0-2-1	27	(701)
0-3-0T	16	(601)
1-2-0	7	(567)
3-0-0	1	(301)

[a] Number of matrices with expected value of 1.000 or greater.

TABLE 14

Comparative Ranking of Triad Types in Davis Data With Theoretical
Rankings R_f and R_g From Least Frequent Triad Type to Most Frequent.

Davis Data	R_f	R_g
0-3-0C, 2-0-1	0-3-0C	0-3-0C
1-2-0C	2-0-1	2-0-1
1-1-1D, 1-1-1U	1-2-0C, 1-1-1D, 1-1-1U, 0-2-1C	1-2-0C
0-2-1C	0-1-2, 0-0-3, 1-0-2, 0-2-1U, 0-2-1D	1-1-1D, 1-1-1U, 0-2-1D
0-1-2	0-3-0T	0-1-2, 0-0-3, 1-0-2, 0-2-1U, 0-2-1D
0-0-3	2-1-0, 1-2-0D, 1-2-0U	0-3-0T, 2-1-0
1-0-2, 2-1-0	3-0-0	1-2-0D, 1-2-0U
0-2-1U, 0-2-1D		3-0-0
0-3-0T		
1-2-0D, 1-2-0U		
3-0-0		

theoretical ordering possible, the frequency of each of these two
triad types is assumed to be the same.

When the theoretical rank orders R_f and R_g are correlated with
the empirical ordering in the Davis data, the Spearman rank correlation coefficient for R_f and the data is 0.92 and the coefficient
for R_g and the data is 0.96. Both coefficients are significant at the
0.001 level. The correlations offer strong additional evidence of
the validity of both orderings. R_g, the ranking obtained by weighting the transitive and intransitive triads unequally, is more highly
correlated with the Davis data than R_f. However, since the unit of
analysis for the test of the Davis data is the collection of matrices
and not individual sociograms, caution must be exercised in draw-
ing conclusions from these results about the success of R_g over R_f.

Discussion

The empirical support obtained by the hypothesized rank orders has significant implications for the transitivity model. By
demonstrating that the concept of transitivity is useful for pre-

dicting the frequency of triad types in sentiment data, the success of the orderings increases confidence in transitivity as an organizing principle of sentiment relations in small groups. The rankings firmly establish balance theory as the conceptual base of the transitivity model and identify the faulty applications of balance theory to triads as the main source of weakness in the model. The success of the orderings suggests that the transitivity model can be improved by formulating a weighted model based on balance arguments applied to triplets.

The confirmation obtained for the rank orders in empirical data suggests a further development of balance theory. The location of the 2-1-0 and 1-2-0C triads in the orderings implies that a certain amount of psychological distress is tolerable in a triadic sentiment relationship. The success of R_f and R_g indicates that inconsistent relationships can be endured if they are balanced by an equal number of consistent relations. These findings add a new dimension to the balance argument which previously was limited to an analysis of inconsistent triplets without including considerations of the countereffect of balanced triplets. Finally, the interaction between consistency theory and the transitivity model outlined in the present chapter illustrates the power of formalization to inform and advance verbal theory.

CHAPTER VI

The Formulation of Weighted
Transitivity Models

In Chapter V arguments from balance theory led to new insights into the nature of transitivity of sentiment in friendship groups. Several propositions were derived establishing a relationship between the balance of transitive and intransitive forces in a triad and the triad's frequency. These theoretical developments can be expressed formally only by weighted models because the unweighted transitivity model cannot distinguish among the triad types on the basis of frequency. The aim of the present chapter is to formulate and test three weighted models based on the propositions in Chapter V. If the weighted models are shown to be more successful in empirical data than the unweighted model, further evidence will have been obtained that intransitivity may occur in sentiment relations if it is balanced by transitivity. The most successful model will provide insight into the way in which balance is achieved.

The Weighted Transitivity Model M_w

The first proposition derived from balance theory stated that the relative frequency of the 16 triad types is related to the number of intransitive triplets contained in the triads. It was predicted that with the exception of 2-1-0, the more intransitive triplets contained in a triad, the less frequently that triad would occur in data. This proposition suggests formulating a weighted model M_w in which intransitive triads are weighted by the number of intransitive triplets contained in them.

Theorem 3 in Chapter I (see page 10) provides the deterministic statement of the unweighted transitivity model. Since the theorem employs triads as the unit of analysis, a corollary based on triplets must be derived to provide the deterministic statement of M_w. Corollary 1 achieves this purpose:

Corollary 1: A directed graph (X, C) is a system of ranked clusters of cliques if and only if it contains no intransitive triplets.

Proof: By Theorem 3, (X, C) is a system of ranked clusters if and only if the graph contains no intransitive triads.

By definition, a triad is intransitive if and only if it contains at least one intransitive triplet.

Therefore, by logical equivalence, (X, C) is a system of ranked clusters of cliques if and only if the graph contains no intransitive triplets.

Since the structures defined by Theorem 3 and Corollary 1 are the same, the transitivity model and M_w differ only conceptually and in their probabilistic versions.

In the stochastic statement of the weighted model M_w, the expected and observed number of each intransitive triad type is multiplied by a weight c_i where c_i is the number of intransitive triplets contained in the triad. The structural index τ_w which measures deviation from the random model is defined in (10) where $T_w = \Sigma c_i T_i$ and T_i is the number of intransitive triads of type i in the graph.

$$\tau_w = \frac{T_w - \mu_{T_w}}{\sigma_{T_w}} \tag{10}$$

The mean and variance of T_w are obtained as follows:

$$\mu_{T_w} = E(T_w) = \Sigma c_i E(T_i) \tag{11}$$

$$\sigma_{T_w}^2 = \text{Var}(T_w) = \Sigma c_i^2 \text{Var}(T_{w_i})$$

$$+ \sum_{i<j} c_i c_j \text{Cov}(T_{w_i}, T_{w_j}) \tag{12}$$

68

Since T_w is a linear combination of T which is normally distributed, T_w also has a normal distribution.

The Weighted Transitivity Models M_f and M_g

Further examination of balance theory led to another proposition regarding the relative frequency of the 16 triad types. While suggesting that the frequency of a triad is inversely related to the number of intransitive triplets it contains, the theory also implied a counterbalancing effect resulting from the number of transitive triplets in the triad. This implication led to the conjecture that the relative frequency of a triad could be predicted by the difference between the number of transitive and intransitive triplets in the triad. An alternate proposition was suggested by the possibility that intransitivity might be a more dominant force in a triad than transitivity. It was conjectured that the order of frequency could be obtained by subtracting the number of transitive triplets in a triad from twice the number of intransitive triplets. The rank orders derived from both of these propositions found support in data. The results showed that the first proposition which assumed that transitivity and intransitivity are opposite but equal forces was more successful.

These two propositions suggest two alternate methods of weighting the transitivity model. The methods consist of weighting the triads by a linear function of the number of transitive and intransitive triplets contained in the triad. The functions f and g described in Chapter V will be used for this purpose, hence, the models are called M_f and M_g respectively.

The deterministic structure described by the models M_f and M_g will be called quasi-transitive graph and defined as follows:

Definition 4: A directed graph (X, C) is quasi-transitive if and only if for every (x, y, z) in X, the intransitivity in (x, y, z) is balanced by transitivity.

In the weighted model M_f the balance condition for a triad is met when the number of transitive triplets in the triad is greater than or equal to the number of intransitive triplets. The weighted model M_g requires that the number of transitive triplets in a triad be greater than or equal to twice the number of intransitive triplets to fulfill the condition.

All of the transitive and vacuously transitive triads satisfy the balance conditions required by M_f and M_g. In addition, the intransitive 2-1-0 triad fulfills the conditions in both models. Consequently, the fundamental theorem for both models can be stated as follows:

Theorem 5:　A directed graph (X, C) is quasi-transitive if and only if it contains no 2-0-1, 1-1-1U, 1-1-1D, 1-2-0C or 0-2-1C triads.

The proof of the theorem is similar to the proof of Theorem 3 and is omitted for that reason.

A quasi-transitive graph is a more generalized structural model than a partially ordered set (poset) because it does not require the absence of the 2-1-0 triad. Since a directed graph must be a poset in order to be a system of ranked clusters of cliques, a quasi-transitive graph only approximates that structure. If the 2-1-0 triads are removed from the graph because of measurement error, as suggested in Chapter V, the quasi-transitive graph becomes a poset. In this case, the deterministic structures of M_f and M_g are the same as the structure of the transitivity model and of the weighted model M_w, namely, systems of ranked clusters of cliques.

In the probabilistic version of M_f the weight d_i for each triad T_i is obtained from the function f where $f(T_i) = t - i$ with t and i representing the number of transitive and intransitive triplets in T_i. The weights are assigned as follows:

for all T_i belonging to (X, C),

if $f(T_i) < 0,\ d_i = -f(T_i)$;

if $f(T_i) \geqslant 0,\ d_i = 0$. (13)

The probabilistic statement of M_g employs the weights h_i obtained from the function g where $g(T_i) = t - 2i$. The triads are weighted in the following manner:

for all T_i belonging to (X, C),

if $g(T_i) < 0,\ h_i = -g(T_i)$;

if $g(T_i) \geqslant 0,\ h_i = 0$. (14)

TABLE 15

Weights d_i and h_i Assigned to Triad Types in M_f and M_g Respectively.

Triad Type	d_i	h_i
0-3-0C	3	6
2-0-1	2	4
1-2-0C	1	3
1-1-1D	1	2
1-1-1U	1	2
0-2-1C	1	2
0-2-1	0	0
0-0-3	0	0
1-0-2	0	0
0-2-1U	0	0
0-2-1D	0	0
0-3-0T	0	0
2-1-0	0	0
1-2-0D	0	0
1-2-0U	0	0
3-0-0	0	0

Table 15 presents the weights assigned to each triad type by these methods.

The structural indices τ_f and τ_g measure the deviation of a sociogram from a random model in the direction of the quasi-transitive graphs M_f and M_g. The indices are defined by (15) and (16).

$$\tau_f = \frac{T_f - \mu_{T_f}}{\sigma_{T_f}} \qquad \text{where } T_f = \Sigma d_i T_i \qquad (15)$$

$$\tau_g = \frac{T_g - \mu_{T_f}}{\sigma_{T_g}} \qquad \text{where } T_g = \Sigma h_i T_i \qquad (16)$$

The mean and variance of T_f and T_g are normally distributed.

The Structural Indices $\hat{T}_{-w}$, $\hat{T}_{-f}$ and $\hat{T}_{-g}$

In order to compare the fit of the unweighted and weighted transitivity models, appropriate structural indices must be defined.

In Chapter III, the statistic $\hat{T}_-$ was derived to measure the approximation of a sociogram to the unweighted transitivity model. $\hat{T}_-$ was defined as follows:

$$\hat{T}_- = \frac{\mu_T - T}{\mu_T - T_{min}} = 1 - \frac{T}{\mu_T} \tag{17}$$

Similar statistics are defined in (18) for the weighted models.

$$\hat{T}_{-w} = 1 - \frac{T_w}{\mu_{T_w}} \qquad \hat{T}_{-f} = 1 - \frac{T_f}{\mu_{T_w}} \qquad \hat{T}_{-g} = -\frac{T_g}{\mu_{T_g}} \tag{18}$$

The indices range between zero and unity with a value of zero implying randomness and unity representing the deterministic structure. $\hat{T}_{-w}$ $\hat{T}_{-f}$ and $\hat{T}_{-g}$ will serve as comparative measures of the approximation of a sociogram to each of the deterministic models M_w, M_f and M_g respectively.

Comparison of the Fit of the Transitivity Model, M_w, M_f and M_g on 51 Groups

The models will be tested in the sample of 51 groups. The first analysis will be a comparison between the fit of the unweighted transitivity model and the weighted models to the data. Since the unweighted model is not sensitive to the interaction between the forces of transitivity and intransitivity in the triads, it is expected that the weighted models will be more successful as evidenced by larger values of $\hat{T}_-$. The second analysis will be a comparison of the fit of the three weighted models to the data. Both M_f and M_g are expected to be more successful than M_w because they take into account a relationship between intransitivity and transitivity in the triads whereas M_w ignores the countereffect of transitivity. M_f is expected to obtain the best fit because it is based on the function f which yielded the most successful theoretical ordering in Chapter V. The results are presented in Table 16 and summarized in Table 17.

In comparing the fit of the unweighted and weighted models to the data, the value of $\hat{T}_-$ for the unweighted model is smaller than the corresponding values for the weighted models in all but one of the 51 groups. These results show that the weighted models are consistently more successful in the data than the unweighted

TABLE 16

Four Measures of Goodness of Fit of Unweighted and Weighted Transitivity Models on 51 Groups.

Group	$\hat{T}_-$	$\hat{T}_{-w}$	$\hat{T}_{-f}$	$\hat{T}_{-g}$	Group	$\hat{T}_-$	$\hat{T}_{-w}$	$\hat{T}_{-f}$	$\hat{T}_{-g}$	Group	$\hat{T}_-$	$\hat{T}_{-w}$	$\hat{T}_{-f}$	$\hat{T}_{-g}$
1	0.647	0.717	0.775	0.777	18	0.382	0.485	0.557	0.551	35	0.274	0.352	0.386	0.396
2	0.416	0.485	0.508	0.509	19	0.336	0.385	0.386	0.397	36	0.366	0.418	0.466	0.465
3	0.416	0.485	0.508	0.509	20	0.485	0.542	0.597	0.600	37	0.278	0.327	0.409	0.396
4	0.485	0.559	0.604	0.606	21	0.254	0.276	0.332	0.324	38	0.342	0.399	0.445	0.447
5	0.605	0.695	0.734	0.728	22	0.369	0.434	0.463	0.468	39	0.362	0.428	0.473	0.481
6	0.324	0.360	0.413	0.408	23	0.474	0.505	0.589	0.582	40	0.371	0.389	0.405	0.407
7	0.428	0.456	0.508	0.509	24	0.222	0.287	0.329	0.330	41	0.656	0.694	0.694	0.696
8	0.465	0.467	0.497	0.496	25	0.345	0.411	0.431	0.439	42	0.395	0.422	0.464	0.457
9	0.267	0.294	0.361	0.358	26	0.368	0.377	0.438	0.422	43	0.555	0.590	0.623	0.632
10	0.228	0.274	0.315	0.313	27	0.550	0.621	0.693	0.688	44	0.394	0.420	0.491	0.482
11	0.462	0.515	0.559	0.562	28	0.509	0.577	0.629	0.625	45	0.445	0.508	0.541	0.547
12	0.424	0.498	0.511	0.514	29	0.321	0.383	0.453	0.451	46	0.428	0.476	0.552	0.547
13	0.442	0.459	0.475	0.478	30	0.148	0.201	0.237	0.238	47	0.700	0.735	0.823	0.815
14	0.274	0.343	0.403	0.399	31	0.358	0.404	0.469	0.461	48	0.391	0.463	0.494	0.503
15	0.220	0.258	0.293	0.298	32	0.314	0.342	0.376	0.376	49	0.175	0.225	0.242	0.251
16	0.234	0.286	0.323	0.317	33	0.348	0.411	0.444	0.446	50	0.243	0.231	0.224	0.230
17	0.605	0.651	0.748	0.652	34	0.319	0.386	0.425	0.427	51	0.266	0.316	0.343	0.346

TABLE 17

Percentage Distribution of 51 Groups According to Rank Order of Four Measures of Goodness of Fit of Model to Data.

Rank Order of Measures of Goodness of Fit	Percentage of Groups
$\hat{T}_{-g} > \hat{T}_{-f} > \hat{T}_{-w} > \hat{T}_{-}$	53%
$\hat{T}_{-f} > \hat{T}_{-g} > \hat{T}_{-w} > \hat{T}_{-}$	43
$\hat{T}_{-g} > \hat{T}_{-f} = \hat{T}_{-w} > \hat{T}_{-}$	2
$\hat{T}_{-} > \hat{T}_{-w} > \hat{T}_{-g} > \hat{T}_{-f}$	2

model. Furthermore, the pattern of success is evident regardless of which method of weighting is used. The results indicate that the weighted sentiment models are more accurate than the unweighted model because they take into account the balance between the forces of intransitivity and transitivity in a triad.

In comparing the fit of the three weighted models, $\hat{T}_{-w} < \hat{T}_{-g}$ in 50 sociograms (98%). Similarly, $\hat{T}_{-w} < \hat{T}_{-f}$ in 50 sociograms (98%). $\hat{T}_{-w}$ is greater than the corresponding statistics for M_f and M_g in only one group (2%). These findings illustrate that the models which weight the triads by combining the transitive and intransitive forces in the triads are consistently more successful in the data than the model which ignores the force of transitivity. In 29 groups (57%), $\hat{T}_{-g} > \hat{T}_{-f}$ while in 22 groups (43%) $\hat{T}_{-f} > \hat{T}_{-g}$. A t-test for matched samples reveals no statistical difference between the values of these two indices in the sample. Consequently, no conclusion can be drawn about the greater success of M_f or M_g.

Discussion

The success of the weighted models over the unweighted transitivity model supports the assumption that the forces of transitivity and intransitivity in a triad determine its relative frequency. By counting only triad types, the unweighted transitivity model is necessarily insensitive to the presence of these forces. On the other hand, the weighted models represent three different methods of relating the forces to triad frequency. The data suggest that assigning weights to the triads on the basis of these forces improves the transitivity model by making it a more accurate representation of the theory of sentimental transitivity.

The better fit obtained by the weighted models M_f and M_g over M_w in the sample suggests that intransitivity is not the only force in a triad determining its relative frequency. There exists a counterbalancing force of transitivity which also influences the frequency of the triads. By simply weighting the intransitive triads by the number of intransitive triplets they contain, M_w ignores the effect of transitivity. The models M_f and M_g assign weights to the triads on the assumption that the force of transitivity as well as intransitivity operate to determine frequency. The success of the models supports this assumption.

While M_g was slightly more successful than M_f in the data, the difference did not attain statistical significance. In Chapter VI the tests of the rank orders R_f and R_g on the sample revealed that R_f received significantly more support than R_g. These results led to the expectation that M_f would be more successful than M_g. Further tests need to be performed on the two models to determine whether one is a more accurate representation of sentiment relations. In addition, the possibility that a different linear or curvilinear function may yield an even more appropriate weighted model must not be excluded. These problems are left for further research.

The results of the tests firmly establish balance theory as an appropriate theoretical foundation for the transitivity model. Focusing on transitivity from a psychological perspective led to insights into sentiment choices which could never have been obtained through a sociological analysis of structure. The weighted model becomes the link between balance theory and the structure of sentiment relations. The success of the weighted models shows that the psychological approach is theoretically sound in contrast to previous efforts to develop the transitivity model as a sociological model of structure and to force it into a psychological explanatory system.

Finally the success of the weighted models has important implications for balance theory itself. The weighted models suggest that a condition under which imbalance in sentiment relations will be tolerated is the presence of a sufficiently strong counteracting force of balance. Establishing conditions under which a theory should hold increases the theory's predictive power. Since balance theory is recognized as having greater explanatory than predictive power, these results attain significance for the development of the theory.

In conclusion, the success of the weighted models forges a stronger link between balance theory and its structural implications. The models correctly locate the transitivity model in balance theory, suggest that the theory be refined when applied to sentiment relations and reveal the alternate patterns which emerge from the modified theory. In this way, the weighted models achieve two of the goals of formalization, namely to facilitate the development of new theory and to establish links between existing theories.

CHAPTER VII

The Structure of Sentiment Relations in Cliques

The final alteration in the transitivity model involves extending the model to permit analysis of the structure of sentiment relations in cliques. In preceding chapters sentiment relations in a group were shown to be transitive and to possess the structure depicted by the transitivity model. In the present chapter the pattern of sentiment relations in cliques will be investigated. It will be hypothesized that the intensity of sentiment experienced by clique members for each other tends to be transitive. Alterations in the data will permit a test of the hypothesis in the sample of 51 groups. If the hypothesis is supported, transitivity will emerge as a more fundamental and pervasive principle in sentiment relations than was previously recognized.

Transitivity of the Strength of Sentiment

The argument from balance theory supporting transitivity of sentiment relations in friendship groups states that the members of an intransitive triad experience psychological distress which impels them to change the bonds and to make the relationship transitive. The same reasoning can be applied to strength of sentiment in cliques. While all the members of a clique are related by mutual positive sentiment choices, any two members may differ in the strength of their attraction to each other. Differences in the degree of sentiment can result in an inconsistent relationship, depicted by an intransitive triad. The discomfort which the inconsistency causes the members will lead them to alter the relationship and make the triad transitive. This reasoning implies that transitivity is an organizing principle of the strength of sentiment relations in a clique.

Fig. 7. Intransitive intensity of sentiment in 3-0-0 triad represented by 0-3-0C triad.

Inconsistency in sentiment relations which differ in strength can be illustrated by considering the triads in Figure 7. Assume that the members of each dyadic relationship in the 3-0-0 triad in (a) are unequally attracted to each other. These differences can be represented by asymmetric arrows in the direction of the better liked person. A possible choice pattern is depicted in (b). One can assume from the choice relations that y is more attractive than x and z is more attractive than y. Therefore, z is more attractive than x and merits a stronger sentiment choice from him. Since x does not experience greater affection for z than z for him, the relationship is unbalanced and x suffers discomfort from the inconsistency. To alleviate his psychological distress, balance theory suggests that x will increase his affection for z which will make the triad transitive as in Figure 8.

Fig. 8. Transitive intensity of sentiment represented by 0-3-0T triad.

Transitivity of the strength of sentiment implies that the pattern of sentiment relations in a clique approximates the structure of the transitivity model. Since only mutual and asymmetric relations are used to depict the strength of sentiment choices, the unweighted deterministic model for these relations is a special case of a poset. The structure is defined by the following corollary to Theorem 3.

Corollary 2: (X, C) is a hierarchy of ranked cliques if and only if the graph contains no intransitive triads and no triads containing null relations.

Proof of the corollary follows directly from the theorem. The absence of N relations limits the graph to one hierarchy and restricts the levels to single rather than clusters of cliques.

Evidence was found in Chapter VI that a weighted transitivity model more accurately describes the structure of sentiment relations than the unweighted model. The formulations of the weighted models were based on propositions from balance theory which suggested that while sentiment relations tend to be transitive, some intransitivity may occur in a graph if it is balanced by transitivity. The deterministic structure of M_g, the most successful weighted model, is a quasi-transitive graph in which every intransitive triplet which occurs is balanced by at least two transitive triplets. Since the same reasoning from balance theory can be applied to strength of sentiment, M_g is a more likely candidate for a structural model of sentiment relations in a clique than the unweighted transitivity model.

In order to test the hypothesis that transitivity is the organizing principle of the strength of sentiment relations in a clique, the fit of both the transitivity model and the weighted model M_g to the data will be examined. Support for the transitivity model will imply that strength of sentiment tends to be transitive and that intransitivity in degree of liking is an infrequent occurrence. Support for M_g will indicate that while strength of sentiment has a tendency toward transitivity, some intransitivity may occur when it is resolved through transitivity. Since M_g is a more accurate representation of the theory of transitivity of sentiment, it is expected to attain a better fit in the data than the unweighted model.

Transformation of the Data

Identification of Cliques. Before the models can be tested on cliques it is necessary to identify the cliques in each group in the sample. A method of detecting cliques is possible with appropriate modifications in SOCPAC 1. The program can be made to list the members of each of the 16 triad types. The members of the 3-0-0 triads are obtained in this manner at the nth choice level. Since some of the 3-0-0 triads may belong to a larger clique, the triads must be examined to determine the maximum number of persons engaged in mutual choice relations with each other. For example, if a five-member clique is present in the group, all the 3-0-0 triads must be found which contain the five clique members. In this way the maximum membership in each clique is determined.

Representation of the Strength of Sentiment Choices. After the cliques have been identified, a matrix of sentiment choices can be obtained for each clique. The entries of the sociomatrix are taken from the larger group matrix which contains the data collected by the new sociometric technique. These entries in the clique matrix represent the ranks which the clique members assigned their best friends on the sociometric tests. In order to introduce hierarchy into this sociomatrix, the entries are converted as follows: whenever $a_{ij} = a_{ji}$, let $a_{ij} = a_{ji} = 1$ and whenever $a_{ij} < a_{ji}$, let $a_{ij} = 1$, $a_{ji} = 0$. The transformation implies that in the corresponding sociogram, sentiment relations of equal strength are represented by mutual arrows, and relations of unequal strength by asymmetric arrows in the direction of the better liked person. Since $a_{ij} = a_{ji} \neq 0$, there are no null choices. The converted sociogram is a more detailed graph of the sentiment relations in a clique and can be used for a test of the transitivity model.

Test of the Transitivity Model and M_g in Cliques

Using the method described above, five- six- seven- and eight-member cliques were obtained from the sample of 51 groups for a test of the transitivity model. Two cliques were found in each of four groups and a single clique in ten groups. The four-member cliques in the sample were eliminated because their structure is less interesting. The frequency of distribution of the cliques according to size is given in Table 18.

Since the distribution of the structural index τ deviates from normal when $g \leqslant 5$ or when $g > 5$ but M and A are small, the sample will be analyzed in two parts. The index τ will be used to test the model on the six- seven- and eight-member cliques, all of

TABLE 18

Frequency Distribution of Cliques According to Size.

Size of Clique	Frequency
8	1
7	2
6	3
5	12

which have relatively large M and A values. The models will be tested on the five-member cliques by employing the descriptive index $\hat{T}_-$.

Table 19 presents the values of τ and τ_g for the six- seven- and eight-member cliques. The results show that τ differs significantly from random ($p < 0.01$) in the direction of the transitivity model for three cliques (50%). In a fourth clique the value of τ could not be obtained because the variance of T was zero, but the clique possesses the exact structure of the transitivity model as revealed by $\hat{T}_-$. Consequently, four cliques (67%) support the transitivity model. In examining the values of τ_g one finds that four cliques (67%) deviate significantly from the random model ($p < 0.01$) in the direction of M_g with one of these cliques possess-

TABLE 19

Values of τ and τ_g for 6, 7 and 8-Member Cliques.

Size of Clique	τ	τ_g
8	−5.69	−4.11
7	−3.74	−2.26
7	−4.55	−2.35
6	−0.35	−1.54
6	−	−
6	−1.18	−1.08

[a] The values of τ and τ_g for this clique could not be obtained because the variance of T was equal to zero.

ing the deterministic structure of the model. The remaining two cliques do not differ significantly from random but examination of the $\hat{T}_-$ values for these two cliques reveals that one possesses perfect structure and the other contains 70% of the maximum structure. This yields a total of six cliques (100%) which support the weighted model M_g.

The values of $\hat{T}_-$ and $\hat{T}_{-g}$ were obtained to test the models on the 12 five-member cliques. Since $\hat{T}_-$ is a descriptive measure of structure, a value of $\hat{T}_-$ must be chosen to define close approximation to the deterministic model. In the present study, $\hat{T}_- = 0.50$ will be used for this purpose. In other words, a graph which contains 50% of its maximum structure will be considered evidence in support of the model. Table 20 presents the results. The findings show that three of the five-member cliques (25%) support the transitivity model. Seven cliques (58%) support M_g, five of which possess the exact structure of the deterministic model.

In summarizing the results of the two analyses on the eighteen cliques, one finds a total of only seven cliques (39%) showing

TABLE 20

Values of $\hat{T}_-$ and $\hat{T}_{-g}$ for Five-Member Cliques[a].

Clique	$\hat{T}_-$	$\hat{T}_{-g}$
1	—	0.10
2	0.089	—
3	0.52	0.786
4	0.20	0.20
5	0.24	1.00
6	0.089	0.40
7	0.662	1.00
8	1.00	1.00
9	0.412	0.51
10	0.089	1.00
11	0.226	1.00
12	—	0.10

[a] In the cliques for which no value of $\hat{T}_-$ or $\hat{T}_{-g}$ is listed, the index is undefined because $T > \mu_T$.

support for the transitivity model while 12 cliques (67%) support M_g. The poor fit of the data to the transitivity model indicates that either strength of sentiment is not transitive or that intransitivity exists but is counteracted by transitivity. The success of M_g supports the hypothesis that strength of sentiment in sociometric relations tends toward transitivity and that some intransitivity in the degree of sentiment in a triad may exist if it is balanced by transitivity.

Additional support for this hypothesis may be obtained by comparing the fit of the transitivity model and M_g in each clique. Table 21 illustrates that $\hat{T}_- < \hat{T}_{-g}$ for every clique in the sample. This implies that M_g is consistently more successful than the unweighted model. These results provide further evidence that in-

TABLE 21

Comparison of Measures of Goodness to Fit ($\hat{T}_-$ and $\hat{T}_{-g}$) of Unweighted Transitivity Model and M_g on 18 Cliques[a].

Clique	$\hat{T}_-$	$\hat{T}_{-g}$
1	0.613	0.936
2	0.444	0.819
3	0.578	0.681
4	0.054	0.706
5	1.00	1.00
6	0.158	1.00
7	–	–
8	0.089	–
9	0.52	0.786
10	0.20	0.20
11	0.24	1.00
12	0.809	0.40
13	0.662	1.00
14	1.00	1.00
15	0.412	0.51
16	0.809	1.00
17	0.226	1.00
18	–	0.10

[a] In the cliques for which no value of $\hat{T}_-$ or $\hat{T}_{-g}$ is listed, the index is undefined because $T > \mu_T$.

transitivity in the strength of sentiment relations can only exist if it is balanced by transitivity.

Discussion

The results indicate that the principle of transitivity not only organizes sentiment relations in a group but also systematizes the strength of those relations in a clique. In addition the success of M_g implies that intransitivity may occur in sentiment choices of unequal strength only if it is balanced by transitivity. These conclusions lead one to believe that transitivity of sentiment is a more fundamental and pervasive phenomenon than previously recognized. Forces exist within a group and again within a clique, independent of the personalities of the members, which constrain and pattern interpersonal choices. The fit of M_g on the data reveals that the configuration of these relationships is a quasi-transitive graph.

The identification of clique members by use of SOCPAC 1 is a simple and accurate method of clique detection. In traditional sociometric studies, cliques were identified visually by use of the sociogram or sociomatrix. Dependence on visual analysis led to inaccuracy. Even when a precise definition of clique was issued, identification by observation was extremely tedious and subject to error. These difficulties made analysis of cliques on a large scale basis virtually impossible. The method of clique identification devised here provides a reliable technique for determining clique membership which can be used in any type of sociometric study.

The method of employing ranked data to introduce hierarchy into the sociogram contains a serious weakness. The technique is based on the assumption that the ranks assigned by the clique members to each other can be compared. In other words, one assumes that if i ranks j as first and j ranks i as second, the i likes j more than j likes i. However, ranking is not based on an interval scale and comparisons between ranks cannot be made without risk of error. The problem of error in depicting strength of sentiment by digraphs is inescapable because the strength of relationships cannot be represented satisfactorily by the presence or absence of an arrow. In the present analysis the danger of error is reduced because allowing ties creates a more meaningful rank order.

The formulation of the method of detecting cliques and depicting the strength of sentiment by digraphs permits an extension of the transitivity model to the analysis of clique structure. This extension maximizes the potential of digraphs to reveal the pattern of sentiment relations. While formerly the model was restricted to the analysis of dichotomous relations, namely, the presence or absence of sentiment, it can now be applied to degree of sentiment. This allows more refined tests of the principle of transitivity. The importance of this extension is revealed by the dominant role played by cliques in group structure.

The aim of Chapter VII was to determine whether intensity of sentiment in cliques is characterized by transitivity. A test of the unweighted transitivity model and of M_g on 18 cliques revealed that transitivity is an organizing principle which determines both sentiment choices and the strength of those choices. The success of the transitivity model in making apparent the non-obvious relationship between transitivity and strength of sentiment illustrates the power of formalization.

CHAPTER VIII

Transitivity in Competence Based Interpersonal Relations

In the preceding chapters it was shown that transitivity is the organizing principle of sentiment relations in friendship groups implying that interpersonal sentiments tend to crystallize into hierarchies of ranked clusters of cliques. One final question remains. Can transitivity explain other networks of interpersonal relations equally well? In the present chapter it will be argued that the extent to which a conceptual base used to map social structure is rooted in consistency theory affects the incidence of transitivity observed in the group. This contradicts the assumption implicit in Holland and Leinhardt's selection of sociograms with different conceptual bases for the initial test of the transitivity model. The proposition will be tested by comparing the fit of the transitivity model to competence data and to sentiment data. The results will provide insight into the generalizability of transitivity in explaining the structure of interpersonal relations.

Previous Studies of Group Structure

The assumption that a single social structure exists in a friendship group can be found in many sociometric studies. These studies imply that any sociometric question will reveal this structure. Bjerstedt (Bjerstedt, 1955) asserts that sentiment (emotional acceptance), competence and power are merely different aspects of one social structure. Sampson (Sampson, 1963) and Homans (Homans, 1961) make the same assumption and offer the notion of status incongruity to support their belief. They claim that individuals possess a tendency to perceive someone viewed as high on one dimension, such as social power, as high on other dimensions too, because it is less costly for individuals to have a more unitary set of expectations for another person than a varied set.

Empirical studies seem to support the assumption of a single structure. Gardner (Gardner, 1956) presents evidence of one structure in his findings that functional leadership, defined as relative influence (power), is directly related to popularity (acceptance). Similarly, in a study of 415 second and fifth graders, Zander and Van Egmond (Zander and Van Egmond, 1958) report that social power is significantly correlated with intelligence. Holding intelligence constant, they find power and attractiveness highly correlated. A relationship between competence and status is revealed in findings by Foote and Cottrell (Foote and Cottrell, 1955) as well as in studies by Homans and Blau (Homans and Blau, 1955).

A number of other studies are based on the assumption that many social structures are present in a friendship group. Glidewell (Glidewell, 1965) posits a multi-dimensional concept of social organization and states that positions of individuals in a social structure can be differentiated along each of several dimensions: status, interpersonal attraction, perceived competence, social power and vulnerability to sanction. Empirical results also support this assumption. Shoobs (Shoobs, 1947) in his study of a classroom of thirty-four children differentiates friendship choices and workmate choices and finds that friendship plays little or no part in the choices of workmates. Grossman and Wrighter, (Grossman and Wrighter, 1948) in sociometric studies of 117 children in four sixth-grade classes, find that intelligence at the median or above has little relationship to acceptance. Lippitt and Gold (Lippitt and Gold, 1959) report a low correlation between emotional acceptance and competence.

While these studies seem to present contradictory findings regarding the structure of a group, in reality they contain little of structural significance. They view social structure as the collection of positions of individuals in a group and measure differences in structure by comparing the number of choices received by group members on two sociometric tests. This approach views interpersonal relations from an individualistic rather than a structural perspective. Focusing on choice totals ignores the underlying patterns of relationships which reveal structure while reliance on visual analysis can hide the kinds of variation in these patterns which imply different structures.

A more promising attempt to study structure was made by Davis and Leinhardt when they formulated the transitivity model. However, the 917 sociograms they used to test the model came from sociometric tests in which a variety of questions was asked. The conceptual bases of these questions touched on power, prestige, status, interpersonal attraction, competence and propinquity. By pooling responses to such diverse questions, Davis and Leinhardt assumed that all interpersonal choice relations, regardless of their conceptual bases, have the same structure. Consequently, while their study employs a rigorous definition of structure and a powerful methodology, it is no more significant than previous ones in detecting differences in patterns of interpersonal relations with various conceptual bases.

The limitations of these studies illustrate the need for a rigorous investigation of differences in the structure of interpersonal relations based on distinct social dimensions. One method of detecting these differences, if they exist, is to test the transitivity model on both non-sentiment and sentiment based sociometric data. If the non-sentiment data have a poorer fit to the model these relations do not possess as strong a tendency toward transitivity. In the present chapter a comparison will be made between the fit of the transitivity model to sentiment data and to data in which the basis for choice is perceived task competence, specifically, perceived competence in science.

Intransitivity in Competence Relations

The rationale for postulating transitivity as the organizing principle of sentiment relations was derived from balance theory. When the choice relation depicted in Figure 3 is sentiment, x finds y's choice of z inconsistent with his own failure to choose z. The inconsistency stems from x's belief that his reasons for liking y are the same as y's reasons for liking z which implies that he should be attracted to z also. The psychological distress caused by the inconsistency prompts him to change the bonds in the triad to make it transitive.

The same argument is less convincing when applied to competence based relations. In the first place, competence can be defined in many ways. One may perceive another to be competent if the other possesses any one of a large number of skills or talents. If the choice relation in Figure 6 were perceived competence, the relationship would be inconsistent from x's perspective. However, x could explain the inconsistency to himself by assuming that his definition of competence differed from y's. By reducing the psychological distress in this way, he makes the intransitivity in the triad tolerable.

One could also argue that the tenets of balance theory are weaker when applied to competence based relations because the activities associated with these relations are more limited and have a shorter duration. To choose another on the basis of competence may require working with him on a specific task but the relationship need not extend beyond that well-defined assignment. In addition, there is no expectation that the association will continue after the task has been completed. On the other hand, choosing another as friend usually involves close association for a long period of time. Since the distress caused by inconsistency in a relationship is more intense the longer the members are in proximity, inconsistency should be more endurable in competence based relations than in sentiment relations.

These arguments suggest that consistency theory does not explain competence based relations as well as sentiment relations implying that the network structures with these conceptual bases will not be identical. This leads to the expectation that sociometric data based on competence will not fit the transitivity model as well as sentiment data. The hypothesis will be tested by comparing the success of the transitivity model on competence and sentiment based sociograms.

The Competence Data

The sample for the test is the same 51 groups used in the test of the transitivity model. The sentiment based sociometric test described in Chapter II was administered first, followed by one in which competence was the criterion. The competence question was set in a hypothetical situation which emphasized the value of the resource. The subjects were asked to imagine that they were to enter a science contest which required doing a science project. They could work on the project with one other class member of their own choosing. The two students who submitted the best project would be awarded the prize.

The subjects were then asked to make a list consisting of the person they would most like to work with on the project, the person they would choose next if the first person were not available, the person they would choose third, and so on, continuing the process until they had listed all the persons they would most like to work with on the project. Following this they made another category consisting of students they would like to work with if no one in their first list were available. Finally, they made a list of anyone in the class whose name was not yet mentioned. When the lists were completed, they ranked the students in each category. The test administrator stressed that ties were allowed, that each category could contain as many or as few names as they desired and that leaving one or more categories empty was also permissible. The same directions for ranking in the last category that were given for the sentiment test were repeated here.

The sentiment and science data were collected on the same day for two reasons. First, administering one test immediately after the other prevented the subjects from discussing their responses between tests. In addition, changes which might occur in the choice relations over time and which would reduce the comparability of the two sets of data were avoided.

On the other hand, the method of administering the sociometric tests may have introduced biases into the data. In the first place, consistently asking the sentiment question before the science question could result in a halo effect. If the subjects possessed a tendency to repeat friendship choices in response to the competence question, the incidence of transitivity might be increased, biasing the data against the hypothesis. Therefore, an observed difference between the fit of the model on the two sets of data must be interpreted as a conservative estimate of the real difference.

A second bias may result from the way the two questions were asked. For the sentiment data, the subjects were told first to select the set of class members who they considered to be their best friends and then to rank the persons in that set. For the competence criterion, they were asked to choose their most preferred science partner, their second most preferred science partner, and so on, until they had listed all the individuals that they would most like to work with on the project. In the first case, the subjects aggregated their responses before ranking whereas in the second test they ranked first and then aggregated. One effect of this procedure may be that a smaller number were chosen for the most preferred category in the science data than in the sentiment data. This bias is eliminated when the first choice level of analysis is used.

Test of the Transitivity Model on Sentiment and Competence Data

The transitivity model was tested on the two sets of data at the first choice level. The structural index τ was calculated to measure deviation from randomness in the direction of the transitivity model in both data sets. Figures 9 and 10 represent histograms of these values. The mean τ-value in the sentiment data is -5.8 and the median is -5.6 while in the competence data the mean and median values of τ are -4.5 and -4.3 respectively. τ is significant $(p < 0.01)$ in 49 groups (96%) in the sentiment data and 45 groups

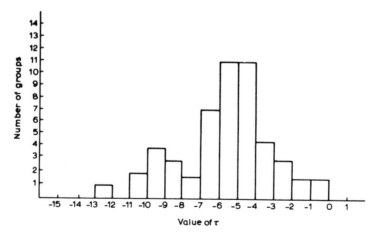

Fig. 9. Values of τ in sentiment data (N = 51).

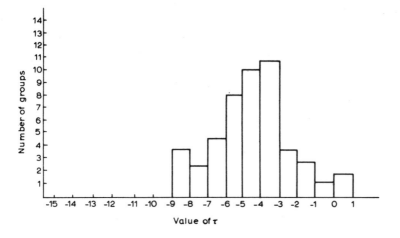

Fig. 10. Values of τ in competence data (N = 51).

(88%) in the competence data. Both samples show a tendency away from randomness in the direction of the model with the deviation from randomness attaining greater significance in the sentiment data.

To compare the fit of the transitivity model with the sentiment and competence data from each group, the values of $\hat{T}_-$ for each sociogram were obtained. Table 22 illustrates these results. In 39 groups (76%) the model is more successful on the sentiment data. Since 50% of the sentiment sociograms are expected to have a better fit to the model by chance, a binomial test reveals that the results lie outside the 0.99 confidence interval. Consequently, the transitivity model is more successful in a significantly larger number of sentiment sociograms ($p < 0.01$) than competence sociograms.

Discussion

The test results indicate that competence relations do not possess as strong a tendency toward transitivity as sentiment relations. As a consequence, the structure of ranked clusters of cliques is not as evident in competence data. Whether another structural model based on a different organizing principle could more accurately describe competence based relations remains to be investigated. A

TABLE 22

Comparison of Measures of Goodness of Fit ($\hat{T}_-$) of Transitivity Model to Sentiment Data and Competence Data.

Group	Sentiment $\hat{T}_-$	Competence $\hat{T}_-$	Group	Sentiment $\hat{T}_-$	Competence $\hat{T}_-$	Group	Sentiment $\hat{T}_-$	Competence $\hat{T}_-$
1	0.681	0.693	18	0.449	0.418	35	0.473	0.614
2	0.514	0.355	19	0.178	−0.006	36	0.445	0.168
3	0.755	0.552	20	0.491	0.482	37	0.400	0.202
4	0.565	0.492	21	0.298	−0.039	38	0.453	0.546
5	0.749	0.373	22	0.265	0.209	39	0.598	0.511
6	0.341	0.304	23	0.472	0.359	40	0.568	0.507
7	0.495	0.287	24	0.219	0.169	41	0.627	0.231
8	0.393	0.363	25	0.414	0.238	42	0.463	0.337
9	0.287	0.254	26	0.433	0.344	43	0.170	0.361
10	0.284	0.463	27	0.545	0.503	44	0.451	0.429
11	0.327	0.387	28	0.572	0.429	45	0.513	0.474
12	0.511	0.304	29	0.306	0.387	46	0.354	0.329
13	0.524	0.427	30	0.500	0.342	47	0.605	0.703
14	0.402	0.352	31	0.438	0.493	48	0.580	0.644
15	0.279	0.262	32	0.489	0.488	49	0.421	0.204
16	0.540	0.062	33	0.457	0.296	50	0.548	0.486
17	0.664	0.493	34	0.370	0.389	51	0.091	0.268

star model seems to be an appropriate candidate to test. For the present, the results provide evidence that the patterns of interpersonal relations based on different conceptual dimensions are not all identical.

Besides providing empirical support for a multi-dimensional concept of social organization, the results suggest placing a requirement on data which are used for a test of the transitivity model. Since not every sociometric criterion yields the same results, it is important to obtain sociometric data rooted in consistency theory which is the conceptual base of the transitivity model. Pooling data from various sociometric criteria may lead to inaccurate conclusions about sentiment structure. Since the Davis-Leinhardt data pool contains sociograms with different conceptual bases, the poor fit which the model obtained in their data compared to the sample of 51 groups may be partially the result of this structural confusion.

Finally, the results point to a theoretical problem that has not been addressed in the present study. It is entirely possible that sentiment itself is a multi-dimensional concept. There are, in fact, studies which support this conjecture. Interpersonal attraction has been associated with propinquity, perceived similarity of attitudes, similarity of belief systems and complementarity of resources (Festinger, Schachter and Back, 1950; Newcomb, 1960; Smith, Williams and Willis, 1967; Gross, 1956). These studies indicate that interpersonal attraction is, at the very least, a complex sentiment and may indeed be built on more than one conceptual base. In the present study, transitivity of sentiment was hypothesized without considering the bases for interpersonal attraction. A next step in the research would be to determine whether refining the criterion of sentiment would reveal more transitivity and provide an even better fit with the model.

In summary, the results obtained in Chapter VIII revealed that the principle of transitivity which organizes sentiment relations into hierarchies of ranked clusters does not characterize all patterns of interpersonal relations equally well. In particular, competence based relations were found to be less transitive than sentiment relations. These findings lend support to a multi-dimensional concept of social structure.

CHAPTER IX

Summary and Directions for Future Research

Science is man's attempt to order his universe to make it understandable. The scientific process involves searching for patterns of
regularity in empirical phenomena and ultimately discovering the
laws which explain these patterns. The physical sciences have long
since taken the lead in this search for order and laws with the
biological sciences more recently attaining prominence. The social
sciences alone remain behind in the effort to posit scientific laws.

By extensive work during the past decade, the social sciences
have come closer to the point where they can justifiably pose
social laws to explain human behavior. Several consistent patterns
of regularity in social phenomena have been discovered. Among
these may be considered the influence of the unconscious on behavior and the role of technology in social change. These dis-
coveries, and others which are generally less dramatic because the
phenomena are familiar, have moved the social sciences ahead in
their attempt to explain social behavior. And following the lead of
the other sciences in which mathematics was found to be a useful
tool in facilitating the discovery and explanation of the laws of
nature, social scientists have begun to employ mathematics to attain this goal.

The discovery of social laws is important for three reasons.
First, knowledge of the laws of human behavior will enable social
scientists to explain and predict patterns of human interactions.

Second, social laws will reveal the influences which constrain human behavior and the implications of these constraints. Finally, by providing a meaningful definition of expected behavior, social laws will clarify the study of deviant behavior.

Recently, psychological consistency theorists have pointed to transitivity as a pattern which characterizes interpersonal relations.[7] They contend that positive interpersonal sentiment tends to be transitive, that is, if A likes B and B likes C then A likes C. Theoretical support for this assertion comes from balance theory which claims that intransitive relations occur infrequently because they are psychologically distressful while transitive relations tend to appear often because they are stressless and satisfying. Substantial empirical support for transitivity of sentiment has been found in sociometric data. In light of this evidence, McFarland (McFarland, 1971) suggests that transitivity, along with other assertions from balance theory, is a prime candidate for the status of social law.

Sociologists have discovered a relationship between transitivity and the structure of interpersonal relations.[8] They have shown that the tendency toward transitivity limits some sentiment relations and increases the likelihood of others. The network of sentiment which emerges under these conditions is a system of ranked clusters of cliques. This structure can be found in all small social systems which are distinguished by transitivity.

The present research aims to shed additional light on the "law" of transitivity of sentiment and its structural implications. The study is built on the work of James Davis, Samuel Leinhardt and Paul Holland who proposed the transitivity (partial order) model as the general structural model for interdependencies in positive sentiment relations. The model implies that if transitivity is an organizing principle of sentiment relations then interpersonal sentiments will tend to crystallize into a structure which can be described as hierarchies of ranked clusters for cliques.

The transitivity model is a promising tool for characterizing social structure because it overcomes the weaknesses inherent in traditional sociometric analyses of structure. By defining structure as a pattern of regularity abstracted from a concrete population, the model avoids the individualistic perspective in traditional studies which incorrectly associates structure with position in the social system. By positing a hierarchical ordering of cliques, it removes the questionable assumption of a mono-clique ideal on which they are based. By providing more precise techniques to detect patterns of sentiment, the model removes the risk of distorting group structure that is inherent in the visual analysis of sociograms.

Despite the improvement of the transitivity model over traditional methods of studying social structure, certain problems had to be confronted before it could be used effectively to study sentiment relations. Among these were the need (1) to reduce measurement error inherent in the previous work, (2) to improve the model's representation of theory and (3) to define an index which permits comparison of groups on the basis of structure and comparison of the fit of alternate models. Without further work in these areas, the transitivity model would inevitably enjoy only limited success in detecting and representing sentiment relations. The present study endeavored to increase the usefulness of the model by resolving these problems.

Traditional sociometric procedures possess a tendency to yield data which distort the underlying group structure they are presumed to represent. In sociometric data obtained from the fixed choice method, discrepancies may arise between a subject's actual number of friends and the number of choices allowed on the test. In addition, structural constraints imposed by limiting the number of choices may severely bias the data against the model. The free-choice techniques may yield data contaminated by an "expansion bias" that occurs when a subject forgets to mention certain group members or by a "response norm" which may affect the number of responses given by a subject who has previously taken fixed-choice tests. Since the only data on which the transitivity model had been tested were a pool of sociograms collected by these procedures, a rigorous test of the model remained to be performed.

In order to reduce measurement error in data collected to test the transitivity model, a new sociometric technique was developed. The method consists of asking each subject to list everyone in the group in one of three categories — "best friend", "friend" or "everyone else". Each individual is allowed to determine his own cut-off point for the first two categories. The subjects are also requested to rank the members within each classification, with ties being permitted. The technique of individual cut-off points reduces measurement error stemming from the discrepancy between a subject's actual number of friends and the number allowed and eliminates the structural biases caused by constraining choice totals. The requirement to list everyone removes the "expansion bias" by bringing into awareness some who would otherwise be forgotten and by increasing the likelihood that such persons are classified as "friends".

Sociometric data collected by the new technique from a sample of 51 children's groups were used for a test of the transitivity model. The model received substantial support in every group. A comparison between the success of the model in the new data pool and in the original one revealed considerably more support for the model in the 51 groups. The fit of the transitivity model in data of high quality provided strong support for the hypothesis that transitivity is an organizing principle of sentiment relations.

The second problem which had to be confronted before the transitivity model could achieve its promise as an effective method of studying sentiment structure was a weakness inherent in the model. The weakness stemmed from a faulty application of consistency theory to triads. The model defines an intransitive triad as one which contains at least one intransitive triplet. It asserts that all intransitive triads are unbalanced and will occur with the same relative frequency. This assertion is not theoretically sound. Balance theory presents consistency as a psychological state of an individual, not the property of a triad; a triad is inconsistent only if one or more members experience it to be so. Moreover, if some triads contain more inconsistency than others, balance theory would predict that they are less likely to occur. Ignoring these aspects of the balance argument and attempting to force predictions about the frequency of triadic structures into a psychological explanatory system makes the transitivity model a poor formal representation of balance theory.

To eliminate the theoretical weakness of the transitivity model, balance theory was applied to triplets rather than to triads. The application generated a rank ordering of triads from the least likely to occur to the most likely. The success of the ordering in the data led to the formulation of three weighted models based on

100

slightly different theoretical considerations. The first model weighted the triads according to the number of intransitive triplets they contained while the weights for the other two models were obtained from linear combinations of the number of transitive and intransitive triplets in each. A test of the models on the sample of 51 groups revealed that the weighted models obtained a significantly better fit in empirical data than the original transitivity model and that the models which assumed that transitivity and intransitivity are counteracting forces in establishing balance were most successful. The weighted models provide a major improvement in the transitivity model by accurately representing the tenets of consistency theory. In addition, they resolve the problem of the too frequent occurrence of the 2-1-0 triad which deprived the model of support.

The final problem associated with the transitivity model was the need of a structural measure for comparisons. Holland and Leinhardt derived an index τ to measure the tendency of a sociogram to deviate from a random model in the direction of the transitivity model. While τ measures significant deviation from randomness, it reveals little about how closely a sociogram approximates the deterministic model. Moreover, since τ is a test statistic and not a measure of relationship, it cannot be used to compare groups on a structural basis or to compare the fit of alternate models.

In order to make possible the kinds of tests for which τ is inappropriate, $\hat{T}$ was defined as a measure of relationship. However, the results needed to calculate $\hat{T}$ are not yet available. A split-range function $\hat{T}_-$ which is easy to calculate and suitable for sentiment data was suggested as an alternative. The index is useful to measure the fit of sociometric data to the transitivity model, to compare the fit of the model in different groups and to determine the relative success of different structural models. In the present study, $\hat{T}_-$ was employed to test the transitivity model in small groups where τ was not normally distributed, to compare the fit of the model in groups under two different sociometric criteria, and to determine the relative success of the weighted models.

By reducing measurement error in sociometric data, by improving the fit between the transitivity model and its theoretical base and by defining a measure of relationship for tests of comparisons, the present research fashioned the transitivity model into a valuable tool for a rigorous analysis of sentiment relations. These efforts pave the way for an extensive use of the model in future studies of social structure.

In addition to improving the transitivity model, the present study utilized the model to explore two aspects of interpersonal relations which had not previously been examined. The first was the intensity of sentiment relations in cliques. It was argued that the psychological distress which a person feels when he is involved in inconsistent sentiment choices is also experienced when the strength of sentiment relations is unbalanced. Consequently, sentiment intensity should tend toward transitivity and possess the structure depicted by the transitivity model.

To test the hypothesis, a method of detecting cliques in a group was derived. When the cliques in the sample of 51 groups were identified, the ranks of the members obtained by the new sociometric technique were utilized to depict strength of sentiment. A mutual arrow was associated with two subjects who ranked each other equally and an asymmetric arrow in the direction of the better liked person with two subjects of unequal rank. The transitivity model and one of the weighted models were tested on these data in 18 cliques. While the transitivity model was only partially successful, the weighted model received strong support. The results indicate that transitivity characterizes the intensity of sentiment relations as well as sentiment choices and that intransitivity in the strength of sentiment relations in a triad tends to be balanced by transitivity. These findings provide a better understanding of the structure of sentiment relations and reveal another application of the principle of transitivity.

The second aspect of interpersonal relations explored by use of the model was the structure of sociometric choices in data with different conceptual bases. An assumption implicit in the selection of sociograms for the initial test of the transitivity model by Holland and Leinhardt was that any sociometric question would reveal the same structure. Since the conceptual base of the transitivity model is consistency theory, it seemed dangerous to assume that sociometric data not rooted in the same theory would possess the structure depicted by the model. To determine whether a network of relationships with a different conceptual base possesses the same structure as a sentiment network, the

102

model was tested on both sentiment and competence based data. A tendency toward transitivity was observed in the competence data but significantly more support was obtained for the model in the sentiment data. The findings illustrate that the extent to which a conceptual base used to map social structure is consistent with balance theory affects the incidence of transitivity observed.

Theoretical Developments

The use of mathematics in the present study to formalize verbal theory and to model social behavior rests on three assumptions. First, mathematics provides a language in which relationships can be expressed more clearly and accurately. Second, mathematical theory can reveal new relationships which extend verbal theory. Finally, the easily manipulated abstract variables in mathematics can facilitate linkages between existing verbal theories. All three assumptions have been corroborated.

The formulation of the weighted transitivity models revealed a non-obvious relationship between transitivity and its structural implications. The theorems established that if sentiment relations are balanced by a requisite amount of transitivity, then the structure of these relations approximates a system of hierarchies of ranked clusters of cliques. The success of the models in high quality data led to a new understanding of the interdependent relations which exist among group members and shed light on the group constraints and interlocking group relations which, along with personal characteristics, determine human behavior.

The use of mathematics revealed a new relationship which has important implications for consistency theory. The success of the weighted models illustrated that intransitivity may occur in sentiment relations if it is balanced by transitivity. By suggesting a condition under which balance holds, these results add a new dimension to the balance argument which presently does not include an analysis of triads containing both consistent and inconsistent triplets.

The transitivity model and the subsequent weighted models established a link between psychological consistency theory and sociological theories of group structure. Balance theory predicts the absence of inconsistency in friendship relations while Homans' theory of social interaction and Blau's theory of social exchange predict the appearance of cliques and a hierarchical order in friendship groups. The graph theorems reveal that each phenomenon implies the other, and consequently, that each theory is strengthened by the other. This linkage makes a multi-theoretical approach to the study of positive interpersonal relations possible. The strong supporting arguments for transitivity of sentiment from different theoretical perspectives provide additional evidence that transitivity may be a scientific law of human behavior.

Directions for Future Research

A number of problems encountered in the present study remain to be resolved. Since solutions to these problems should improve the transitivity model and provide better statistical techniques for testing it, they become important areas for future research.

The calculation of T_{max} for a given sociogram is a major problem associated with the structural index $\hat{T}$. Two methods of obtaining T_{max} were suggested. The first of these is to find the distribution of τ for each sociomatrix. The maximum value of τ for the distribution, when standardized, would yield T_{max}. However, since the calculation of the exact distribution of τ, even for small groups, is extremely tedious, an attempt to estimate T_{max} may be more productive. An alternate method is to devise an algorithm for calculating T_{max} for each graph. Obtaining T_{max} manually or through computer analysis for groups containing a small number of mutual, asymmetric and null relations may offer suggestions for a technique which would yield an exact or approximate value in larger groups. A related problem inherent in the calculation of T_{max} by any method is the determination of the appropriate constraints to place on a sociogram before obtaining the measure.

A second problem introduced by the use of the structural indices τ, $\hat{T}$ and $\hat{T}_-$ was the need for a more appropriate random model. While the distribution used to calculate the values of the statistics in the present study is suitable for sociometric data, a better model could be obtained by fixing choices made, choices received and mutual choices. By controlling for the skewed distribution of sociometric choices, the new model would increase confidence in the validity of the structural indices. The mathematical results needed to implement this random model have still to be derived.

A final question remains regarding the appropriate weights for a weighted transitivity model. Both the function f and g yielded rank orders and weighted models which received substantial support in the data. While the rank order R_f was more successful than R_g, no statistical difference was observed between the fit of the weighted models M_f and M_g. Alternate linear and perhaps curvilinear functions need to be tested to determine which function most closely expresses the relationship of balance between transitivity and intransitivity. A regression analysis on the sample of 51 groups should provide a likely candidate for this function.

Besides the methodological problems stated above, a number of substantive issues arise from the study. Not the least of these involves the pervasiveness of sentimental transitivity. Leinhardt (Leinhardt, 1968) found that transitivity characterized children's friendship relations and showed that the tendency toward transitivity increases with age. Holland and Leinhardt (Holland and Leinhardt, 1972) discovered transitivity in both children's and adult groups. The present work detected transitivity in every group in a sample of sixth- seventh- and eight-grade classes. Further study of sentiment choices is needed, particularly in adult groups, to determine how extensive transitivity is in positive interpersonal relations and under what conditions it can be expected. Research of this nature is particularly necessary if transitivity is to be posited as a social law.

By providing a method of rigorously analyzing sentiment structure, the transitivity model opens the door for extensive research in this area. The numerous sociometric studies of children's groups can now be supplemented by more sophisticated analyses of the determinants and consequences of social structure. The results may stimulate renewed interest in sociometrics as a guide to psychotherapy. In addition, traditional studies of organizations which generally only focus on the effect of organizational variables on individuals as members of formal or informal groups can now be extended to an investigation of the effect of organizational variables on group structure. A cursory glance at the relationship between classroom organization and sentiment structure in the groups used in the present study reveals that the sentiment structure of the groups in flexible classroom arrangements more closely approximated a system of ranked clusters of cliques. The model will also permit analyses of the effect of sentiment structure on individual and group variables such as morale, syntality and productivity.

In its present formulation, the transitivity model is a static model which pictures social order at one point in time. Since social order is a process which unfolds over time, greater understanding of social interaction may be obtained by use of a dynamic model. The transitivity model could be transformed into a dynamic model by use of probability theory. A more productive method might be to replace the graph-theoretic approach by an alternate mathematical theory.

A dynamic model may provide balance theorists with new insights. The weighted models developed in the present study revealed that the force of intransitivity can be counteracted by transitivity to produce a new state of balance. A dynamic model could reveal the stability of this state of balance over time as well as the kinds of changes which are likely to occur. The model may also be of value to educators. Since faculty and student groups form and re-form annually, an understanding of the development and stabilization of structure in these groups may suggest methods of structuring groups for maximum effectiveness.

While graph theory has provided well-defined concepts and powerful theorems to facilitate the study of sentiment structure, the usefulness of digraphs in modeling social behavior is limited. Some of its weaknesses, such as the inability to depict strength of sentiment, have been illustrated in the present study. To express the wealth of information contained in sociometric data and to reveal complex patterns of relationships beyond the triad will probably require more sophisticated mathematical theories. The structure of algebraic theory and non-metric geometry make them reasonable candidates for more powerful models of sentiment structure.

Transitivity has been postulated as an underlying principle which organizes positive interpersonal sentiment relations. The results of this empirical study provide further evidence that transitivity of sentiment tends to be a pervasive characteristic of sentiment relations. The study also demonstrates that the structure of sentiment relations can be described accurately by explicitating the structural consequences of transitivity.

Footnotes

1. Complete citations are given in Glidewell's bibliography.
2. An equivalence relation is one that is reflexive, symmetric and transitive.
3. See, for example, Leon Festinger and H. Hutte, "An Experimental Investigation of the Effect of Unstable Interpersonal Relations in a Group", *Journal of Abnormal and Social Psychology,* XLIX (1954), 513-522; R. Tagiuri, "Social Preference and Its Perception", in *Person Perception and Interpersonal Behavior,* ed. by R. Tagiuri and L. Petrullo (Stanford: Stanford University Press, 1959); W.M. Wiest, "The Quantitative Extension of Heider's Theory of Cognitive Balance Applied to Interpersonal Perception and Self Esteem", *Psychological Monographs,* LXXIX, No. 14 (1965).
4. For a further discussion of this point, see R. Abelson *et al., Theories of Cognitive Consistency: A Sourcebook* (Chicago: Rand McNally, 1968), p. 548. Philip Bonacich used Homans' theory to argue for transitivity of sentiment. He claimed that in a triad where there are positive relations between p and O_2 but a negative relationship between O_1 and O_2, that the positive sentiments will lead O_1 and O_2 to interact frequently with p and *vice versa.* But when both are in p's company, they will be thrown together in an uncomfortable situation. To relieve the discomfort they will change the relationship with p or their feelings about each other. For this reason, unbalanced sentiment triads are unstable. This argument differs slightly from consistency theory because it suggests that it is the physical presence of the parties to the negative relations that causes discomfort, not any inconsistency in the relationship itself. The argument can be extended by pointing out that even when there is a null rather than a negative relationship between O_1 and O_2 they will be thrown together because of interaction with p. This causes them to interact with each other. Interaction, according to Homans, increases sentiment and this changes the sentiment structure of the triad.
5. The technique of individual cut-off points was suggested by R. Darrell Bock, Department of Education, University of Chicago.

107

6. Samuel Leinhardt and Robert Dryfoos wrote a Fortran IV program, SOC PAC1, which computes τ in addition to performing other sociometric analyses. The author is grateful to Professor Leinhardt for providing this program for the present study.

6a. The probabilities were derived by Robert Fay, a graduate student in the Department of Statistics, University of Chicago.

7. A review of the literature including citations for empirical studies on transitivity of sentiment is found in Davis, "Social Structures and Cognitive Structures", *Theories of Cognitive Consistency: A Sourcebook* (Chicago: Rand McNally, 1968), pp. 544-550.

8. A comprehensive review of the work of Davis, Holland and Leinhardt in this area is included in the bibliography.

Bibliography

Books

Abelson, Robert; Aronson, Elliot; McGuire, William; Newcomb, Theodore; Rosenberg, Milton and Tannenbaum, Percy. *Theories of Cognitive Consistency: A Sourcebook.* Chicago: Rand McNally, 1968.

Bjerstedt, A. *Interpretations of Sociometric Choice Status.* Copenhagen: CWK Gleeup, Ejnar Munksgaard, Lund, 1955.

Blau, Peter M. *The Dynamics of Bureaucracy.* Chicago: University of Chicago Press, 1955.

Blau, Peter M. *Exchange and Power in Social Life.* New York: Wiley and Sons, 1964.

Coleman, James S. *The Adolescent Society.* New York: Free Press of Glencoe, 1961.

Cook, W.W.; Leeds, C.H. and R. Callis. *The Minnesota Teacher Attitude Inventory.* New York: Psychological Corporation, 1951.

Coombs, Clyde. *A Theory of Data.* New York: Wiley and Sons, 1964.

Festinger, Leon. *A Theory of Cognitive Dissonance.* Evanston, Illinois: Row Peterson, 1957.

Festinger, L.; Schachter, S. and K. Back. *Social Pressures in Informal Groups.* New York: Harper and Row, 1950.

Foote, N.N. and L.S. Cottrell. *Identity and Interpersonal Competence.* Chicago: University of Chicago Press, 1955.

Glidewell, John C.; Kantor, Mildred B.; Smith, Louis M. and Stringer, Lorene A. *Social Structure and Socialization in the Elementary School Classroom.* Report of a workgroup to the Committee on Social Science Research Council. The St. Louis Country Health Department. Clayton, Missouri, 1965.

Gordon, C. Wayne. *The Social System of the High School.* New York: Free Press of Glencoe, 1957.

Harary, Frank; Norman, Robert Z. and Cartwright, Dorwin. *Structural Models.* New York: Wiley and Sons, 1965.

Hollingshead, August B. *Elmtown's Youth.* New York: Wiley and Sons, 1949.

Homans, George C. *The Human Group.* New York: Harcourt, Brace and World, 1950.

Homans, George C. *Social Behavior.* New York: Harcourt, Brace and World, 1961.

Nadel, Siegfried. *The Theory of Social Structure.* London: Cohen and West, 1956.

Newcomb, Theodore M. *The Acquaintance Process.* New York: Holt, Rinehardt and Winston, 1961.

Sherif, Muzafer and Sherif, Carolyn. *Groups in Harmony and Tension.* New York: Harper and Row, 1953.

Whyte, W.H. *The Organization Man.* New York: Simon and Schuster, 1956.

Articles

Abelson, R.P. and Rosenberg, Milton J. "Symbolic Psycho-logic: a Model of Attitudinal Cognition", *Behavioral Science,* III (1958).

Blake, R. *et al.* "Housing, Architecture and Social Interaction", *Sociometry,* XIX (1956), 133-139.

Bonney, M.A. "A Study of Social Status on the Second Grade Level", *Journal of Genetic Psychology,* LX (1942), 271-305.

Bonney, M.E. "The Relative Stability of Social, Intellectual and Academic Status in Grades II to IV and the Interrelationship Between these Various Forms of Growth", *Journal of Educational Psychology,* (1943), 88-102.

Cartwright, Dorwin and Harary, Frank. "Structural Balance: A Generalization of Heider's Theory", *Psychological Review,* LXIII (1956), 277-293.

Coleman, James S. "Academic Achievement and the Structure of Competition", *Harvard Educational Review,* XXIX (1959), 330-351.

Davis, James A. "Clustering and Structural Balance in Graphs", *Human Relations,* XX, No. 2 (1967), 181-187.

Davis, James, A. "Clustering and Hierarchy in Interpersonal Relations: Testing Two Graph Theoretical Models on 742 Sociomatrices". *American Sociological Review,* XXXV, No. 5 (October, 1970), 843-851.

Davis, James A. "Social Structure and cognitive Structures", *Theories of Cognitive Consistency: A Sourcebook.* Ed. by Robert Abelson, Elliot Aronson, William McGuire, Theodore Newcomb, Milton Rosenberg and Percy Tannenbaum. Chicago: Rand McNally, 1968, pp. 544-550.

Davis, James A. and Leinhardt, Samuel. "The Structure of Positive Interpersonal Relations in Small Groups", *Sociological Theories in Progress.* Ed. by Joseph Berger. Boston: Houghton Mifflin, 1972.

Festinger, Leon and Hutte, H. "An Experimental Investigation of the Effect of Unstable Interpersonal Relations in a Group", *Journal of Abnormal and Social Psychology,* XLIX (1954), 513-522.

Gardner, G. "Functional Leadership and Popularity in Small Groups", *Human Relations,* IX (1956), 491-509.

Gross, E. "Symbiosis and Consensus as Integrative Factors in Small Groups", *American Sociological Review,* XXI (1956), 174-179.

Grossman, Beverly and Wrighter, Joyce. "The Relationship Between Selection, Rejection and Intelligence, Social Status, and Personality Amongst Sixth Grade Children", *Sociometry,* XI (1948), 346-355.

Gullahorn, J. "Distance in Friendship as Factors in the Growth Interaction Matrix", *Sociometry,* XV (1952), 123-124.

Hallinan, Maureen. "Comment on Holland and Leinhardt", *American Journal of Sociology,* LXXVIII (May, 1972), 1201-1205.

Harary, Frank. "On the Measurement of Structural Balance", *Behavioral Science,* IV (1946), 107-112.

Heider, Fritz. "Attitudes and Cognitive Organization", *Journal of Psychology,* XXI (1946), 107-112.

Holland, Paul and Leinhardt, Samuel. "A Method for Detecting Structure in Sociometric Data", *American Journal of Sociology,* LXXV, No. 3 (November, 1970), 492-513.

Holland, Paul and Leinhardt, Samuel. "Some Evidence on the Transitivity of Positive Interpersonal Sentiment". *American Journal of Sociology,* LXXVII (May, 1972), 1205-1209.

Holland, Paul and Leinhardt, Samuel. "Transitivity in Structural Models of Small Groups", *Comparative Group Studies,* II (May, 1971) 107-124.

Holland, Paul and Leinhardt, Samuel. "The Structural Implications of Measurement Error in Sociometry", *Journal of Mathematical Sociology,* 3, 1, 85–112.

Kogan, N. and Tagiuri, R. "Interpersonal Preference and Cognitive Organization", *Journal of Abnormal and Social Psychology,* LVI (1958), 113-116.

Leinhardt, Samuel. "Developmental Change in the Sentiment Structure of Children's Groups". *American Sociological Review,* XXXVII, No. 2 (April, 1972), 202-212.

Lippitt, R. and Gold, M. "Classroom Social Structure as a Mental Health Problem", *Journal of Social Issues,* XV, No. 1 (1959), 40-58.

Long, N.J. "An Explanatory Study of the Relationship Between the Growth of the Whole Child and an Attempt to Improve the Social Power of Sociometrically Rejected Elementary School Children", *Dissertation Abstracts,* XIX (1958-1959), 482-483.

Merton, R.K. "The Social Psychology of Housing", in *Current Trends in Social Psychology.* Ed. by W. Dennis and A. Lippitt, Pittsburgh: University of Pittsburgh, 1948, pp. 207-209.

Newcomb, Theodore M. "An Approach to the Study of Communicative Acts", *Psychological Review,* LX (1953), 393-404.

Osgood, C.E. and Tannenbaum, P.H. "The Principle of Congruity in the Prediction of Attitude Change", *Psychological Review,* LXII (1965), 42-55.

Sampson, E.E. "Status Congruence and Cognitive Consistency", *Sociometry,* XXVI (1963), 146-162.

Shoobs, N.E. Sociometry in the Classroom", *Sociometry,* X (1947), 154-164.

Smith, C.R., Williams, L. and Willis, R.H. "Race, Sex and Belief as Determinants of Friendship Acceptance", *Journal of Personality and Social Psychology,* VI (1967), 127-137.

Tagiuri, R. "Social Preference and Its Perception", In *Person Perception and Interpersonal Behavior.* Ed. by R. Tagiuri and L. Petrullo. Stanford: Stanford University Press, 1959.

White, H. "Management Conflict and Socio-economic Structure", *American Journal of Sociology,* LXVII (1961), 185-189.

Wiest, W.M. "The Quantitative Extension of Heider's Theory of Cognitive Balance Applies to Interpersonal Perception and Self Esteem", *Psychological Monographs,* LXXIX, No. 14 (1965).

Zander, A. and Van Egmond, E. "Relationship of Intelligence and Social Power to the Interpersonal Behavior of Children", *Journal of Educational Psychology,* XLIX, No. 5 (1958), 257-268.

Unpublished Materials

Leinhardt, Samuel. "The Development of Structure in the Interpersonal Relations of Children". Unpublished doctoral dissertation, University of Chicago, 1968.

McFarland, David D. "The Role of Mathematics in the Recent Development of Sociology". Paper presented to the annual meeting of the American Association for the Advancement of Science, Philadelphia, December 26-31, 1971.

Index